José Miguel Cejas

MONTSE

A fun-loving teenager

José Miguel Cejas

MONTSE
A fun-loving teenager

SCEPTER

London   Princeton

Nairobi   New Delhi   Singapore

This edition of *Montse — A fun-loving teenager* is published:
in England by Scepter (U.K.) Ltd, 21 Hinton Avenue, Hounslow, TW4 6AP;
in the United States by Scepter Publishers Inc., PO Box 1270, Princeton, NJ 08542;
in Singapore by Scepter Publishers (Singapore), 10 Pasir Panjang Close, Singapore 118969;
in India by Scepter, P. O. Box 4009, New Delhi 110 017; and
in Kenya, by Scepter Ltd., P. O. Box 28176, Nairobi.

This is a translation of *Montse Grases – Biografía breve*, first published in 1994 by Ediciones Rialp S.A., Madrid, and in 1999 by Scepter.

ISBN 0 906138 46 9

Cover design & typeset in England by KIP Intermedia, and printed in Singapore.

Contents

week's leave. Just a week – not a day more. Then you come straight back."

A few days later Manuel Grases managed to get to Barcelona, having crossed the Ebro in a barge as the bridges were all blown up. The wedding was organized with haste. He and Manolita Garcia arranged for Fr. Ricardo Falp, an old friend of the family to marry them on August 7 at 11 a.m. in San Severo's, a small baroque church near the Cathedral.

At 11 a.m. sharp Manuel was at the door of the church in his freshly ironed Lieutenant Engineer's uniform. At 11:10 Manolita had not arrived. It was the usual delay. However...

At 11:15 Manolita had still not appeared; at 11:30 still no sign. After a wait of three years! 11:45: what could be wrong?

"Nothing was wrong," Manolita commented laughing, "except that there was only one big mirror in my mother's house and my sister, my cousins, and I all had to get ready in front of it. Between one thing and another by the time I got to church – in my hat and my navy blue suit – it was midday. An hour late. Just one little hour..."

After the wedding they went to Burgos in Castile on their honeymoon. They got there on August 8 and the following day Manuel carried out a promise he had made to our Lady if he survived the war, to go from Burgos to the Carthusian monastery of Miraflores, walking barefoot, praying.

And this is where our story begins. A simple story in which suffering and happiness, sorrow and joy, love and pain intermingle.

It is a story of how happiness can come from suffering, sorrow can give rise to joy, and how pain can be turned into love.

1

A large family

When we have twelve...

When his week's leave was up, Manuel returned with Manolita to his military post in Benicarlo; from there he was posted to Valencia. As soon as Manuel got his longed for demobilization, they moved to Barcelona and set about finding an apartment.

At last they found one to their liking. It was on the first floor of a house on Paris Street in a part of Barcelona called the "extension." It was a relatively large apartment, though Manuel considered it a bit small because they were thinking of having a good number of children.

"True," said Manolita. "I remember saying: 'Let's not argue about how many children we are going to have. After we have twelve we will discuss it.'"

They furnished the house in part with Manuel's parents' furniture. They had died when he was a child and their furniture had been carefully stored by his uncle and aunt for years. Among the belongings there was an object of particular interest. It was an image of Our Lady of Montserrat that had been vandalized by some militia during the war. Manuel recalls: "We had it restored, and it turned out fine. We put it in a place of honor in our new apartment so that she would bless our home...."

"Soon," Manuel continues, "I found a job in the Productos Pyre plant, which was in the suburb of Pueblo Nuevo. I worked on the expansion of the plant buildings. As the factory was a bit far out I bought a motorbike: a 250 cc 'Matchless'. And thus we started to get on our feet.

"The children began to arrive... Enrique was the first one. He was born on May 17, 1940, after a long and painful labor. As soon as he was born I remember asking our Lord to grant him some kind of vocation as I always dreamt that my children would give themselves to God.

"A vocation. Some kind of vocation... although I always had one special dream: to have a son who would be a priest...."

Montse

It was the beginning of the forties, those years immediately after the Spanish civil war, which had ended in 1939, those terrible "hungry years." They were the years of shortages and hardship, black marketeering and food rationing, power cuts, a single electric hot plate and paraffin cookers, cars fueled by compressed gas, water restrictions and ration cards. "I had a tobacco ration card and another for gasoline for the motorbike. I was allowed five liters a month, which I stretched as far as possible with benzol from the factory, taking care that it would not crystallize in the carburetor in wintertime," Manuel recalls.

"They were years of great joy too. In the summer of 1941, God willing, we would be four in the family. And God was willing. One day in July our second child was born. A girl. Montse."

Manolita recalls: "She was born on July 10, 1941, looking at the sky. She was baptized Montserrat by Fr. Javier de Olot on the 19th in the parish of Our Lady of the Pillar.

"As was the custom we gave her several other names: Amelia in honor of Manuel's maternal aunt and Margarita for her godmother, Margarita Vellvé. However at home we always called her simply Montse.

"She was a delightful child. Later on, when she was older, Montse would say to me jokingly that it was thanks to my having breastfed her for nearly fourteen months that she was a bit chubby.

"But she never had a complex about being stout, despite her brothers teasing her often; she would joke to me, 'Can't you see, Mommy. Who asked you to nurse me for such a long time?'

"I repeat she never did have a complex, nor should she have had one, although a bit plump, she was not at all fat.

"When she was small her eyes were blue. They got darker as she got older and at the end were dark brown with very dark eyelashes. From an early age she showed herself to be a lively character."

God wanted more of her

Two years later, in 1943, the Grases home suffered its first trouble. Little Montse became very ill.

Manolita says: "At first it did not seem to be anything serious. She had an attack of asthma, which our family doctor, Dr. Moragas, did not make a fuss about. He reassured me, though he did say it would last for weeks. However, as the asthma was very distressing and it seemed to go on for so long, we decided to get a second opinion. We consulted another doctor, with a very good reputation, and then our worries really began!

"The new doctor prescribed a cough medicine with a high codeine content. This dried up the saliva so much that she contracted capillary bronchitis, which became very serious indeed, so much so that the doctor said to me one day, 'Has she not died yet? I don't understand how she can cope.' The doctor was the problem. He refused to recognize he had made a wrong diagnosis.

"Oh dear. When we went back to Dr. Moragas

and he saw her condition, he said to her: 'Poor little thing! What a state you are in!'

"Thank God, she was back in Dr. Moragas care. He prescribed one saline drip after another and expectorants for the bronchitis. She was breathing so heavily you could hear her from the far end of the house.

"The danger period lasted for about a month. We sat by her side night after night. At this time I was on the verge of giving birth to Jorge.

"I remember that every time Dr. Moragas came to see Montse he would ask me about my pregnancy.

'Not yet, Madam?'

"And I would say, 'Is Montse out of danger yet?' I was sure I would not give birth until Montse was well again.

"He delayed answering me for days and days, until one day he checked her and said:

'Well, I like that better.'

'Is she out of danger?'

'I am not saying that much,' he answered, prudent as ever.

"I remember the night when her illness reached its crisis. My sister, Ines, and her husband, a doctor, spent the night with us. They were sure she would not last the night and did not want us to be alone. 'Lie down and rest, don't worry, you need to rest,' they said to me, as I was in the late stages of pregnancy and had spent many sleepless nights....

"Naturally I refused and stayed by her bed

sewing some clothes for the new baby. My sister and my brother-in-law were in our room – where Montse's bed also was. They were sitting on my bed, but sleep overcame them. Manuel also fell asleep, I don't remember where.

"I was sewing and looking at Montse... and now and again I would put a cool cloth on her forehead to wipe off the sweat and I changed her pillow. It was the middle of winter.

"During the night I saw that she was improving, I remember perfectly the moment the improvement came. I thanked God many times for leaving her with us.

"When my sister and her husband woke up and saw her smiling they were happily surprised. Later my sister told me she never thought that Montse would last the night. Darling Montsina! God wanted more of her!"

Fresh air

As a consequence of Montse's illness the Grases went to Seva, a little village near the city of Vich about 40 miles north of Barcelona, for the summer. "We went there because the doctor suggested that we find a place where Montse could breathe fresh air. We took an old terrace house at the entrance to the village. Thanks be to God, Montse got well quickly and soon she was blooming with good health.

"We loved Seva, so much so that we decided

to return. The children could run around freely, and it was tranquil and peaceful."

They spent some pleasant and restful months there. "Our family life was typical of any family of the 'heroic and long-suffering middle class,' as my father used to call it," Manolita recalls.

At the end of the summer of 1943 they went back to Barcelona. The family album has many pictures of those days, similar to those of many Spanish families of the time. There are also photographs of a house in Vallvidiera where they spent some summers, photos of Manolita and the children out for walks in the parks of Barcelona, as well as family celebrations of weddings and christenings, Ignacio's for instance, their fourth child who was born the following year on October 25, 1944.

"Those photos of little Montse reflect her character very well: cheerful, jovial, very playful, and with a bit of a temper!

"It is a strange thing: When I try to recall that time all I can remember are some amusing anecdotes. I am telling them because they reflect Montse's character right from her early days. For instance, on one occasion she took part in a song festival of Llongueras at the Music Palace. Llongueras was a well-known composer of children's songs at the time. The song title was *El joc del cel,* and Montse sang it barefoot dressed up as an angel. She looked very sweet; but, oh dear... she had to remain seated for quite some time on the stage waiting for the others to get through their performances. After a while she got restless– I can see her now – and what should occur to her, in front of all those people, but to pick her toes!

"I am telling you this because some people expect to find something extraordinary about her right from childhood and, as can be seen from these photos, Montse was a child with the same likes and dislikes as other little girls of her age. She was not 'a holy child'; people are not born saints but become saints....

"Sometimes people ask Manuel and me: 'What kind of Christian education did you give Montse for her to...?' I always reply: 'The same formation as we gave the other children...' We did not do anything differently. Of course, we did try to instill a Christian way of life in them... We taught them what we believe and struggle to put into practice. For instance, we taught them, right from the cradle, to say some simple prayers, to develop a relationship with the Child Jesus, to have devotion to our Lady, to accept and offer up pain, to struggle against one's own little defects, to help each other...."

Manuel intervenes: "I used to insist on one point in particular that I think is basic: sincerity." "Tell me what happened," he would say to them after some mischief. "Look, I don't mind if you have broken this, that, or the other; what I want above all is that you are sincere, that you tell the truth always, no matter what. If you lie to me, then indeed I will punish you."

"Yes, we gave her a Christian upbringing... but what happened in Montse's soul," Manolita concludes, "was because God wanted it. It was the result of her correspondence to grace... the fruit of God's grace and love."

By 1946 the older children were already at school in Barcelona. Enrique went to the Christian Brothers' school at Bonanova and Montse to the nuns of Jesus and Mary.

"I can see her now," Manolita recalls, "running out of the house wearing her uniform, braids flying, down the stairs two at a time, leaning to one side because of the weight of her school bag, with such *joie de vivre*..,"

The Jesus and Mary School had prestige and tradition. It was very well known by Barcelona families. "She loved her school. At the beginning we sent her as a day student. One of the nuns who knew her, Mother Anne, who was Procurator at the time, told me years later how she remembered her perfectly because 'Montse had made an impact on her'."

First Holy Communion

Meanwhile the Grases family was growing. In 1947 Manuel and Manolita had been married eight years and already had five children. Enrique, Montse, Jorge, Ignacio, and the baby, Pilar, who was born in October. Five strong, healthy children, playful and cheerful, who kept their parents on their toes, doing economic wizardry to balance the family budget. Manuel and Manolita were able to prove the Spanish saying that "God supplies the bread for each new mouth." The Grases children, like any others, enjoyed playing cops and robbers, and getting into mischief at their summer home in Vallvidiera. They quarrelled with each other twenty times a day, and twenty times made up again. They would dream about swimming in the sea during the wintertime and at Christmas time they would look forward to "Santa Claus" bringing them an electric train. They would eagerly await the coming of May and their First Communion day as they grew older....

In 1948 Enrique and Montse were going to make their First Communions. Both their parents and their schools had prepared them with special catechism classes. Enrique made his on May 6 at the La Salle School. Three weeks later it was Montse's turn.

It was a very special day. A big feast day with its last minute rush and scramble. Manolita tried on the broad silk lace mantilla with a high comb in front of a mirror while Manuel, already formally dressed, looked nervously at his watch. The older children helped the little ones to dress and comb their hair. When they began to get nervous, their father would remind them of the proverb "make haste slowly." At last when all was ready they set out dressed immaculately. What joy! It had to be like that. It was Montse's First Communion.

There was a festive air at the school. All the lights in the chapel were on and the altarpiece, our Lady holding the Child with arms outstretched, sparkled. The inscription underneath the image read *"Monstra te esse Matrem"* – "show yourself to be our Mother."

The organ struck up its first majestic chords in the choir loft, amid glittering red and gold. Everyone stood and the Mass began....

"After the ceremony we came home," recalls Manolita, "and celebrated together. We had a simple children's party with clowns making merry and telling jokes. It was an unforgettable day... When it was all over my uncle, Mauricio, asked Montse what she had liked best. She answered immediately, 'The clowns!'"

❀   ❀   ❀

" I have mulled over this reply of hers more than once, and it seems to me quite natural that she should have said this. But from then on there were no more clowns on First Communion days so that the children could be more attentive to the only important thing: receiving our Lord in the Blessed Sacrament for the first time.

Everything about Montse was like that: completely normal. She never did anything 'spectacular.' She got close to God very gradually, identifying herself with him little by little, step by step, along the path of little things....

"It is normal for a child of her age to act like this and not to have visions or anything like that. Although, if she had had a vision, for example, I would have understood it as a gift freely given by our Lord. But her life was always a matter of grace and daily struggle, a constant falling in love with our Lord, and an effort to overcome herself in big things and little ones; in everything: in her life of piety, in her dealings with others, with her character... yes, her character above all, because she was clearly very lively."

"She had the character of a very lively little girl," her father qualifies. "Nothing more. Aside from that she was very balanced, joyful, and simple. She was always calm. Well, almost always."

The "almost" refers to Montse's little tantrums. Nonetheless, from what her parents say, the volcanic flames from that Etna with braids were nothing beyond the normal sparks that fly between brothers and sisters in domestic scuffles. And, within a few minutes, that childish fire turned to a lava of laughter, games, and competitions, as happens in any large family...

A clear, candid gaze

Until 1948 there were more boys than girls in the Grases family: three against two; Enrique, Jorge and Ignacio versus Montse and Pilar. But the following year the tables were surprisingly turned. On May 3, 1949, twin girls were born: María Cruz and María Jose. Now there were four girls and three boys. Seven children, each with their joys and sorrows, with their little problems and their characters.

"Montse was very straightforward...," her mother recalls. "She had no guile of any kind... For this reason some girls her age kept her at arm's length, because they did not dare to speak of certain things in front of her.... And she did not understand it. Oh dear, Montse! How hard it was for me to explain life to you !

"It really was difficult for me. Manuel constantly urged me and reminded me of my responsibility towards her; he tried to do the same with the boys.

"I preferred to do it in stages, no mention of storks or such nonsense, but adapted to her age, clearly in the most natural way, avoiding unnecessary details, and with a supernatural spirit. The first question occurred to her at school while reading the Hail Mary. Her classmates started to doubt their mothers when they heard the explanation given in class. As soon as she came home she told me about it because she trusted me implicitly.

'Look, Mom, what it says here: "Blessed is the fruit of thy womb." What does it mean? Some girls were reading this and not understanding it, and they asked me what it meant.'

'What did you say?'

'I said I would ask you and they should ask

their mothers. But they answered that if they did that, they would get into trouble. The best thing would be for me to explain it to them after you had told me.'

"I remember clarifying her ideas and insisting emphatically that the other girls should ask their mothers, who should be the ones to explain these things anyway, and that there was no reason for her to get involved.

"A few days later I asked her:

'Montse have you thought about what we were discussing the other day?'

'No, Mom.'

'Really Montse! Haven't I given you something to think about? Don't you have a single worry?'

'No.'

'Well listen! I want you to promise me something. If you feel the slightest curiosity about what I've said, tell me and we will discuss it further. Is that okay?'

'Yes, Mom.'

"And we left it at that. I have always been thankful to God," Manolita concludes, "for the great trust we had in each other, and I have often thought how important it is for parents to be real friends to their children, to anticipate their big problems and their little ones....

"Montse had a very happy childhood. She did not have any special problems. Apart from her illnesses, all the memories I have of her early years are happy ones."

The memories are simple and intimate, typical of any Christian family of the time. "We always celebrated Palm Sunday in a big way," Manolita continues. "The little ones used to love it! On the day before, their godmothers would bring a palm branch for each of the children, we would leave them all ready in the hall. Then on Sunday morning we would be the first ones in the neighborhood out with our palms. The girls would wear their best dresses, and the older boys, Enrique for instance, would wear the baggy trousers that were in fashion then.

"In Catalonia, the godfather gives a present of *mona de pascua*, a typical pudding that we normally eat after Holy Week, at Easter time like an Easter cake. The children would look forward to this treat. As we knew they were going to get several, we would encourage one of them to give his or hers to some needy people. It was one way, which we thought suitable to their age, of teaching them the virtue of charity, to be generous with something they found a bit difficult.... We used to do the same with Christmas presents.

"However, with respect to the Easter cake, we would give them total freedom: they could give it away or not, though we did encourage them to be generous. So we would take them to the orphanage of St. John of God to visit the sick children or to the St. Raphael girl's orphanage. When Enrique was born we gave a donation in his name to the St. John of God orphanage. We did the same for the St. Raphael orphanage on Montse's birth."

At boarding school

Manolita continues: "Rosario was born in September 1950. We had eight children now. They were strong and healthy, thank God. When they were small I used to take the children to Dr. Moragas if they were ill. Apart from being a good doctor he was a fine person; a man of few words and not given to making long visits. He would treat normal illnesses, like measles and whooping cough, by telephone. He would stop in later, have a quick look, and as he was going out the door, he would tell me what else to do.

"Nevertheless, when I telephoned him one day in October 1950 to tell him that María Cruz, who was just over a year old, had been waking up the previous nights crying, and the doctor of Vallvidiera had not found anything wrong with her but I had observed she would not lean on her right foot, he interrupted:

'Tell your husband to come and fetch me at once, Madam.'

'Don't bother to come Doctor,' I said, 'we will take her to you because she has no fever.'

'Don't worry about me. Just tell your husband to come for me.'

"It was polio. The doctor said the best medication was a peaceful environment. The noise and commotion of the other children was not conducive to her recovery. So we dispatched the older ones to boarding school; the boys, Enrique and Jorge, ages ten and eight respectively, to La Salle de la Bonanova and Montse, who was nine, to the Jesus and Mary School of San Gervasio.

"What could we do? We had no alternative. We had to decide within two days....We labelled their clothes and off they went...."

❁   ❁   ❁

"However in spite of my misgivings, Montse really had a great time as a boarder in the Jesus and Mary School! Every time I now pass by the school door, I remember her playing there in the play-ground wearing the uniform, which suited her so well, or telling me stories of the small room where she slept and where she felt so much at ease. With-out doubt, she spent some very happy years in the Jesus and Mary School....

"She had completely recovered from her first serious illness and was the picture of health.

"This is all I can remember from those years. Thanks be to God in spite of our worst fears, Crucina began to get well.

"I can see now that God was preparing Montse gradually, with these minor problems, for what he was going to ask of her later on. Without straying a whit from what was apparently ordinary."

The Dominicans

Manolita continues: "In October 1951 we moved Montse to the Dominican School, which was nearer home, in Travesera de Gracia, as a day pupil. Thank God Crucina was well enough that it was not necessary for the older children to stay on as boarders. Besides, as Montse was now ten years old, she could go to school and come home by herself....

"I am sure she was very sorry to change schools, not because she was unhappy with the Dominicans, but rather because she had been very happy in the Jesus and Mary School. Here she revealed a character trait: she never once gave the slightest indication of displeasure."

Holy Child Jesus School, more widely known as the Dominicans, had about 800 students in 1951. Ana Vallejo, a contemporary of Montse there, remembers her playing ball during the short morning break, her chestnut hair, cheerful expression, and natural talent for all kinds of sports. She does not stress any particular characteristic though; she was just another student at the school where there were many representatives of big families just like Montse, and where one could still feel the pinch of the lack of material goods during the postwar years.

Roses and thorns

Meanwhile the country at large was slowly recovering from the wounds of the war. The radio was the daily loudspeaker of the social changes. As the years went by it reported the end of rationing, Spain joining UNESCO, the death of Stalin, the coronation of the Queen of England, the successes of the Spanish cyclist Federico Martin Bahamontes, "King of the Mountains"; all of it enlivened by the songs of the popular Jorge Negrete who would belt out from under his wide Mexican sombrero in his powerful voice:

When a Mexican loves
There is no love like his love.

Montse grew up happily, unperturbed in the midst of this changing world, although now and again there would be a little thorn.

Her father recalls: "Once, when she came home from school, she told me she had shown a drawing she had done the previous day, to her teacher. The teacher had told her that the drawing was not hers and that she was a liar and a cheat. She had of course been humiliated. I asked her what she had done. 'Nothing,' she replied. She had not attempted to justify herself...."

She finished sixth grade in June 1953. Despite changing schools, her marks improved. She got honors in Music and Family Formation, failed dismally in Literature, and got good grades in all the other subjects. She also attended the Music Academy and got honors in Piano with distinction in Music Theory.

There was one school activity that she particularly enjoyed, her mother recalls. This was teaching catechism to children in one of the working class suburbs of Barcelona, an activity organized by her teachers. "I remember she used to go often on Sundays, so enthusiastically. She would take them toys, books, and candy...."

Maybe a yearning for God was making itself felt in her soul. Even if this were so, in itself it would not be anything very extraordinary. It is quite likely that many of her classmates at that time also dreamt of self-giving to God. Generous longings of this nature were relatively frequent in the heart of Christian families like the Grases, which were the seedbeds of vocations for the Church and where the ideals of sanctity and self-giving took root from an early age.

A Christian home

The Grases household was a Christian one without being clerical. God took pride of place; however this did not mean saying rosaries continuously. Their way of life was no different from many other Spanish Catholic families. Every morning there would be the usual yawning of the youngest ones, at least one lie-a-bed till the last minute, as well as the hustle and bustle of jobs to be done, school bags to be got ready, and breakfast to be eaten. Manuel Grases left for work early, and the children came downstairs one after the other. They scrambled onto the school bus and peace reigned once more. Now it was time to wage war on the house, sweeping and washing up. Encarna Ramos, a young woman from Cañete de las Torres, a village near Cordoba, helped Manolita diligently with the household tasks.

The morning flew past. Manolita took advantage of this oasis of peace to go to Mass and later, with the help of Encarna, she attended to Rosario, the baby. Between the two of them they cleaned the house, made the beds, and prepared lunch while half-listening to the radio. The radio was an old Telefunken "Southern Cross" model. Concha Piquer was the popular singer of romantic ballads of the time. Sometimes she would be longing for a sailor who had gone to sea; at other times, she would have them laughing with her "girl of the station."

. .Watching the trains go by
was all her elation.
In the town they called her
The girl of the station!
Good-bye, have a good journey
farewell, have a good time
Give my love to all the family
Write me soon in rhyme.

After lunch when Manuel went back to work and the children to school (except on Thursday), Manolita would usually find time to say the rosary or pay a visit to the Blessed Sacrament in a nearby church. Then more domestic tasks with Encarna, and, often enough while they were sewing, they would tell each other the latest jokes, which Pepe Iglesias "the fox" had told the day before on a radio program that began: "I am the fox, the little fox, for the old and the young."

At this time of the day you could hear the confused echo of sighings and wailings: "Carlos... Nita..." (through the patio). Not to worry. It was just the umpteenth episode of the long running radio serial, "That Which Never Dies," with each episode always finishing at the most exciting moment... Manolita did not follow these soap operas, considering them a waste of time. Besides, the afternoon, with its peace and quiet, just flew by. At 5.30 the children would be home again. It was like an invasion: playing, laughing, leaping about, wanting their snack before getting down to their homework until dinner time. And then more fun and games all over the house until bedtime. Only then, at last, did Manuel and Manolita get to sit together in the living room to chat for a while with a bit of peace.

Before getting into bed the Grases children always said the prayers their mother had taught them. "My God, protect us and give us peace." Montse used to say a very simple prayer, "My God, make me good, Enrique too."

As the years went by her prayer required increasing memory; "My God make me good," Montse would pray every night, "and Enrique and Jorge and Ignacio and Pilar and Crucina, and María Jose and Rosario too."

Sanctity in marriage

Manuel explains: "Both Manolita and myself had been trying for years to live a Christian life, and we had included some specific habits. For instance we went to Mass often and we made a retreat every year. People used to say that we were doing enough with what we had on our plate.... However, I felt a deeper longing in my soul– how can I put it? – to do something more for God. How or where could I do this? I had never heard of Opus Dei, although the Work was physically very near me....

"It happened as follows: When we were in Vallvidiera we often saw a couple who lived in the Vallvidiera Hotel walking past, on the Tibidabo road, outside our house. Sometimes a very tall priest would be talking to them. Later on I got to know that the priest was Fr. Emilio Navarro.

"One day quite casually I mentioned this to José Cusó Abadal, a friend of mine, and he thought they were probably making a retreat given by an Opus Dei priest.

'What is that?'

"He gave me a simple explanation and told me a cousin of his, Fr. Juan Bautista Torello, was an Opus Dei priest. I got the idea from this conversation that only celibate men and women could belong to Opus Dei.

'What a pity there is nothing like that for us married people,' I said."

❀   ❀   ❀

What Manuel Grases did not know was that married people could belong to Opus Dei, a way of

seeking sanctity in the midst of the world, by sanctifying work and one's ordinary duties as a Christian.
It had been founded in Madrid on October 2, 1928,
by Blessed Josemaría Escrivá who was beatified in
1992.

From November 25 to 30, 1948, the founder
had given a retreat in Molinoviejo, a conference
center near Segovia, to fifteen married men who
were preparing to belong to Opus Dei. It was the
start of an apostolate in which thousands of men and
women from all over the world would undertake the
task of sanctifying their family lives, making their
dwellings into "bright and cheerful homes" as
Blessed Josemaría used to say.

"I had not heard of Opus Dei, either, but just
like Manuel I felt the need to give more, without
knowing how," Manolita says.

A strange blessing from God

During those years, God had bestowed his
blessings abundantly on the Grases family. He had
blessed them with eight children, and gradually their
financial situation improved. Manuel had set up a
machinery warehouse that brought in a good
income. However, God wished to bless them further.
He sent them... an almost total collapse of the business. A strange blessing, the reader will think. However, Christians know that when God permits economic difficulties it becomes, like pain or illness, a
sign of special favor. And frequently it has this
characteristic: from a human point of view it seems

to come at the worst possible moment.

"It was all the result of disloyal competition in the business, which brought us to the brink of bankruptcy in a very short time. It came when a lot of the children were older and we were paying for private schools...."

The Grases children, not understanding exactly what was happening, saw how their parents struggled to live up to their responsibilities to their staff, sometimes exceeding the demands of justice, in a way proper of practicing Christians.

"Even though we could not afford it," Manolita recalls, "we did not want the children to change schools, as they were getting not just a good human and academic education but a good religious formation too. We thought their education was a priority. We knew from experience that God does not close one door without opening another. And in both schools they gave us all kinds of help."

"I shall never forget one particular morning...," Manuel recalls. "We had an urgent debt due and did not know how to confront the situation. We had tried our best; we had sold the car and gave up the help Manolita had in the home. She had to cope alone with eight children. I was besieged by debts.

The situation was awful. We did not know where to turn....That day we threw ourselves on the mercy of God. I prayed, 'My God, you know we don't know what to do and we have eight children....'

"At that precise moment the postman came

with a check for 40,000 pesetas. Some relatives of
mine from Manresa had died, and I had not even
known of their existence. The executor of their will
had sent me the check. This helped us to trust in God
always, no matter what...."

Happy years

"In spite of the economic problems I have
very happy memories of those years," Enrique, the
eldest, says. "We were a big, happy, fun-loving but
well-ordered family. Our parents insisted on our
practicing the virtue of orderliness, in regard to the
use of our own things and taking care of our books.
The fact that money was scarce helped to make us
more responsible. So our parents did not have to be
constantly nagging us – 'What is that ball doing in
the hall or why are your socks thrown around the
room?'

"The virtue of order meant that though there
were many of us and there was very little money, we
were able to cope.

"Now, with hindsight, I appreciate having
been born into a big family, as a pleasant, enriching
experience. You get used to sharing everything. You
don't have 'your' room, it is always 'our' room.
Especially for us older ones, Montse and I, who
were entrusted with the care of the little ones. The
situation made us more mature and taught us to be
responsible for other people all the time.

However, big families do have a problem.

Being so many it is easier to become independent. Knowing this our parents taught us to be united above all, to perceive the family as a communal enterprise. Each one of us had to contribute his share to support the family, so, when problems did arise, they were divided by eight and we were never overwhelmed.

"This was a gradual process. As we grew older we began to realize how tight the economic situation really was and how much our parents were sacrificing themselves for us. This encouraged us to work better at school, not to ask for unnecessary things, but rather to be happy with what we had.... For instance, I could see how my friends at school had pocket money to buy ice-creams or candy or to play table football. I knew that if I wanted to play this game, which I loved to do, I would have to use the money I had for my streetcar fare.

"This taught me to appreciate that money has to be earned and to understand from an early age that even though it is easy to ask for things, one cannot ask for everything. I began to appreciate the few things I did have and to savor them. Nowadays people do not realize this. Many parents mistakenly consider they have to give their children whatever they ask for, otherwise they will be 'traumatized.' The opposite is nearer the truth. My experience was certainly hard and by comparison with my schoolmates quite arduous; but well worthwhile in the long run.

"In this sense my family was a model of austerity. I have always given thanks to God for not having been able to sail through life, thinking only of my own enjoyment, and pleasing just myself.

"We were a happy family but we were not a 'perfect family.' There are no 'perfect families.' There were aspects of the running of the home in which Montse and I, being the eldest, were not in agreement. I can remember us setting up a kind of family council. It was very funny. It took place on Saturdays. There was a general get-together where we would talk and discuss the running of the home. They were small, unimportant things but from a young person's perspective they appeared crucial – whether we were allowed to do this or that.... Sometimes we got what we asked for... but not always. However, we did appreciate the freedom and trust our parents gave us to discuss everything and to speak our minds at any time."

2

Llar

Rosa Pantaleoni

Some years earlier, another girl from Barcelona, Rosa Pantaleoni, was confronted with the first problems of adolescence. They were physical problems. She had suffered from polio in both legs at the age of eight. Now, having spent several years in a wheelchair, she found herself forced to walk with the aid of crutches. She had one bad arm as well.

"I got to know Opus Dei at a critical moment in my life," she says. "It was in the early fifties and because of my physical state, I thought I had every right to feel miserable... until one day I was talking to Fr. Florencio Sanchez Bella, a priest of Opus Dei from whom I had spiritual guidance. I said:

'Fr. Florencio can't you see how miserable I am?'

'Miserable, eh? Why on earth? Don't you love

other people?'

'Yes,' I answered timidly.

'Is it that you can't do things for others?'

'Yes, I can'

'Well then,' he said forcefully, 'what need have you to think about other things? You know how the Father says that the happiness of heaven is for those who know how to be happy on earth.'

"I was greatly encouraged and thinking about how the words 'the happiness of heaven' made me very happy.

"I met the Father – Blessed Josemaría Escrivá – years later when I was already a member of Opus Dei. It was a very cold day at the Barcelona airport where he had to stop over. Three of us, members of Opus Dei, went there to greet him. I was very young and at first a bit shy…. As soon as he saw us he came forward smiling.

'Hello, Father. My name is Rosa Pantaleoni and I am going to study Pharmacy.'

"He answered in a jocular tone, 'Ah yes, my daughter, you are going to be an apothecary.' Then, in a tone of voice that meant I should always remember it, he added: 'In the dispensary you can do a great work of apostolate. Always remember that I told you, you can do a wonderful job there.'

"I shall never forget how kind the Father was to me or the lovely things he said while making the sign of the cross on my forehead. He told me I had always to be very cheerful….

'Of course, Father,' I said. 'Of course I am

happy. I have my vocation, which is the best thing in the world, and besides, I have had the good luck to meet you!'

"The others from Llar who had accompanied me were surprised at my boldness. But then the Father did not intimidate one, he did not cut one short... just the opposite. He urged me to keep going, to struggle, as if nothing was going to happen, and then we said good-bye. I recall that he then gave me a deep look of affection, and I have treasured this glance of the Father ever since ..."

Llar

What is Llar? As Rosa says, "It is a Center of Opus Dei, at the top end of Muntaner Street, very near Adriano Square; it is for doing apostolate with young women. It began in a small way. They were so hard up in that house that on many days they did not have enough for the bare essentials. Everything was so unpretentious!

"It was a small simple apartment but cozy and pleasant at the same time. There was a laundry room with a big table, a fairly small sitting-room, and a few more rooms. There were no benches in the oratory. We used to kneel on those individual kneelers with rush seats; when you turned the kneeler around, you sat on the rush seat. However, in spite of our lack of means, the oratory was beautiful, it was decorated in warm tones and had a very respectable tabernacle with amber-colored oil lamps. There was also a very pretty image of our Lady, and the floor was so clean that it sparkled!

"There was a confessional in the ante-oratory. Fr. Amadeo Aparicio, a priest of Opus Dei, looked after our spiritual needs. He came to celebrate Mass, to hear confessions, and to preach. Fr. Emilio Navarro and Fr Florencio Sanchez Bella also came during those years. It was also Fr. Florencio who looked after the apostolate in Vich and Gerona, two other cities of the region.

"On Saturday afternoons the priest would give a meditation in front of the Blessed Sacrament. Lots of girls came. On Thursdays there was another meditation for university students. After the meditations there would be a get-together where we would sing, chat, tell stories, laugh a lot, and play the guitar in a warm family setting typical of the spirit of Opus Dei.

"There were also lots of talks on human and spiritual development. Once a month there was a day of recollection for girls who worked as domestics. A lot of young people came to these different activities, mostly students from Barcelona and from nearby towns: Vich, Gerona, Tarrasa, Sabadell, and Badalona...."

The difficulties of the early days

Roser Fernandez recalls: "Those who lived in Llar at that time suffered real poverty. I was not a member of Opus Dei then and like lots of others who went to Llar, I was curious to know where the girls who lived there slept. One night I stayed on in the oratory after everyone had left. When I finally came out, the only people there were the ones who lived there. On my way out I overheard María Casal, who thought they were alone, say from the room next door:

'Not to worry. If the blankets don't come to-night, we won't go to bed. We will stay in the laundry and leave the heater there on. At least that way we will be able to sleep.'

"I was really shocked. To make up a bed they just spread out the blankets and the sheets on the floor... when there were blankets of course.

"This was a real discovery for me. Now I could understand why they did not turn on the central heating. They had no money and the heating cost a lot; winter had come and they had no blankets. Later on I found out that on that particular night they were expecting a present of some blankets.

"That was how I made my discoveries. Another night I saw what they were having for dinner: Spinach with spinach. There was no money for anything better. It was then that I spoke to some other students who attended cookery lessons. Though we were young and did not handle much money, we would bring tins of food from home and leave them lying about the kitchen in Llar as if by accident....

"What was amazing was the elegance and

human dignity with which they accepted the situation, so much so that some of the girls who attended the activities there never noticed. For instance, I can remember one occasion nearing Christmas, one of the students suggested we buy them a picture or a tray... until Digna beckoned to me and without mincing words said:

'Look Roser, what we really need here is a hamper. Now that would be really useful!'

"These situations of extreme poverty are not the norm in Opus Dei where each one supports herself with her work. These were special circumstances that often appear when a Center is being set up, and thanks be to God are quickly solved. The founder went through similar circumstances when he was beginning the Work. However, I shall never forget that. Those women taught me how to confront material difficulties with human elegance and supernatural vision.

"I have such happy memories of that period! For some time we gave catechism classes with Rosa Barrica in the Salud de Badalona area as well as in a school in a shanty town called Montjuich. It was less a school than a shed, rather like those used by workmen to keep their tools in. The children came from very poor families.

"One of the fruits of our Christian formation from Llar was frequent visits to poor people. When I think of the children at Cottolengo; it is as if I could see them now. We gave them lunch, we cut their nails, we washed them....

"Some women – housewives and mothers, members of Opus Dei and their friends – would go to the Turó district, a very poor suburb of Badalona, to teach catechism and attend to the needs of these people who lived in really pitiful conditions. It was a shanty town, constructed from pieces of old wood by the people themselves. It was at the edge of a dusty road among boulders and hollows caused by the rain. They set up a dispensary with the help of some cooperators of Opus Dei and later on a second-hand clothes' shop for the local people. Many such apostolic centers were started with the help of housewives and mothers like Manolita, Montse's mother, who came to know the Work at about that time."

Just what I was looking for

"I got to know Opus Dei through Manuel. A short time previously he had come into contact with Fr. Emilio Navarro," Manolita says. Manuel recalls: "It happened in the simplest way. One evening we were having dinner with a married couple, friends of ours, when we began talking about Opus Dei. I used to think, as you know, that married people could not join the Work, and what they told me was of great interest. So much so that I asked them who could inform me properly. They gave me an address on Atenas Street. I was met there by a priest. It was Fr. Emilio Navarro, the one I had seen going up and down the street in front of Vallvidiera tower a village about 30 miles west of Barcelona where there was a retreat house... I told him about my spiritual longings and he suggested I do a retreat in Vilafranca del Penedés."

Fr Emilio continues the story: "At the time we were beginning the apostolic work with married men; some of them did not understand the constant teaching of the founder of Opus Dei that marriage is a divine vocation and a way to sanctity. But Manuel Grases was one of those who did understand and asked for admission very quickly as a super-numerary of Opus Dei on October 1, 1952, the eve of the anniversary of the foundation of the Work."

"This is what I had been looking for, for years," Manuel said. "In the Work I was reminded that human love and married duties are part and parcel of my Christian vocation, that marriage is a divine way on earth; that my primary apostolate should be in my own house, making it 'bright and cheerful' with my wife and children, that I had been called by God from all eternity to achieve divine love through human love...

"It was a fabulous prospect, something I had always been searching for! They also pointed out a specific mission that I had as the father of a family: to lead my children to heaven, to sanctity...

"I was introduced to Alfonso Balcells, a Catalonian doctor, a lively persuasive character. He gave a talk on spiritual matters in my own house to me and other fathers, some members of Opus Dei and their friends.

"Sometimes Juan Jimenez, a professor from the faculty of medicine in Barcelona, gave the talk. Whether it was Juan or Alfonso who spoke, the themes were prayer, sanctifying our ordinary work, the apostolate, truly loving our wives – 'even being in love with their defects as long as they are not an offense against God', as the founder taught us – and of making every effort to educate our children well... When the talk was over and everyone had gone, I would tell it all to Manolita and she became very enthusiastic."

"On hearing the talks through Manuel," Manolita says, "I decided to get in touch with the women of Opus Dei for myself. I spoke to Fr. Emilio Navarro and he suggested I make a retreat. As I said before, I used to make a retreat every year... however, that year was quite different. I was pleasantly surprised by the positive and optimistic supernatural tone in which the spiritual themes were presented. For instance, when the priests spoke about transcendent matters in the meditations, or about virtues in the Christian life, or about a Vatican document, they always related it to ordinary every-day life. I loved that.

"They talked to us about being saints in our daily lives. They said we had to sanctify ourselves in our own homes with our children, where God wanted us....

"What happened to Manuel happened to me! I immediately thought, this is just what I have been looking for! I realized that Opus Dei presented sanctity in the Christian life as something achievable, as an ideal all of us could aspire to: old and young, priests and lay people, married and single. I understood this was what God was calling me to and... I decided to join the Work."

Such a vision

Some months later, in October 1954, Manolita Grases rang the doorbell of Llar. She was accompanied by her eldest daughter. "I went to fetch her after school and took her to Llar," Manolita recalls. "The flat was several blocks higher up the hill, not far from our house, about twenty minutes walk. Mirufa Zuloaga, the director, welcomed us. Pepa Castelló showed us around and introduced us to the girls who were there at the time."

Pepa says: "That particular day we were hanging some pictures in the corridor when Montse was introduced to me. I remember asking her to lend me a hand and she agreed. Her mother left and she stayed behind to help me." Mirufa Zuloaga recalls: "She was a very pretty, friendly girl, full of smiles." Rosa continues: "She was wearing the school uniform of the Dominicans. The ribbon in her hair was loose and she stood there looking at us a bit doubtfully. I can see her now.... They introduced us. She listened while I played the piano and then I asked her:

'Would you like to learn how to play?'
'Yes I would. I'd like to learn to accompany

songs and that kind of thing.'

"And off she went cheerful and happy, having lost that little doubt she had when she came in."

Her mother recalls: "When she came home that night she was delighted with herself. I think her heart was stolen from her the very first day."

❀   ❀   ❀

Rosa recalls, "From that day she continued coming to Llar fairly regularly, particularly on Saturdays when we had a meditation. She quickly made friends with everyone. She had the gift of knowing how to make friends as her behavior was simple and friendly. She had loads of friends, at school, in Seva... and she loved them a lot."

María Luisa Suriol underlined these qualities and adds: 'But you would not say on seeing her, this girl is a saint, because she did not stand out in anything in particular. She was an ordinary girl, though a delightful one."

Pepa adds: "Many of her friends began to come to Llar thanks to Montse, and we organized a series of talks on spiritual and human formation for them. We spoke about sanctifying work, offering up their classes, their hours of study, about having a personal relationship with our Lord in prayer, about the Christian meaning of mortification, and how to be contemplatives in the midst of the world. We also spoke about some of the human virtues like sincerity, loyalty, cheerfulness...."

Rosa recalls Montse's profound simple gaze. "Her gaze! With that look she would say everything!" Carmiña Cameselle adds: "It was the most fetching thing about her. It was a clean serene look like the girl herself, although she had a bit of a temper. Her father said she was a live wire!"

Rosa concludes: 'That is true. She had a winning manner and was very lively at the same time. She was tremendously spontaneous. She did not like to be contradicted. She got cross quickly if she was teased. So I used to enjoy teasing her, as she would get rattled at once.

"Not that she had a bad temper. She was an extrovert – with a touchy side that came to the fore now and again. One day I said: 'Look, we have been on an excursion. But we did call you at home first, and they told me you didn't want to come.' 'What do you mean that I didn't want to come. Of course I did. You didn't call at all.' She was quite upset. 'Whoa, Stop!' I said, trying to calm her down, 'it was only a joke.'

"...I remember her so well leaning over the piano keys with such a smile... always cheerful and happy.... Right from the beginning she understood that cheerfulness is a basic trait of the spirit of Opus Dei.

"She was fun-loving. She was so bubbling with life and health that it was a joy to be by her side. She was not a gossip and did not like tittle tattle. She knew how to defer to others and to trust them. She had an innate sense of justice – she would get upset if she discovered that someone had cheated by not paying for their ticket on the train....

"Above all she was a sportswoman. She was always talking about her tennis matches, her climbing excursions up Montseny a mountain range about 30 miles northeast of Barcelona, her friends... and she loved the theater. I recall her at a session of theater readings of 'The Mayor of Zalamea.' I am not certain but I think she took the part of the Mayor...."

"She had a great relationship with her mother," Carmiña Camesclle recalls. "She discussed everything. They got along famously. A glance was enough for perfect communication."

"She was very, very generous," Rosa concludes. "She had many splendid human qualities. She identified herself with the spirit of Opus Dei and became very enthusiastic with the ideal of being a saint in the middle of the world, sanctifying work, and helping others on the road to sanctity. We used to talk a lot about apostolate and about calling our friends to the sacraments. I would say: 'Just think. Maybe the only opportunity that friend of yours has of hearing about God is when she is with you. Taking her to listen to the priest and to confession is very important... and you have to help her.'

"She started to take her classmates to Llar, and also her friends from the Seva group. She always had apostolic zeal, long before recognizing her vocation to Opus Dei.

"She realized very clearly the economic hardship we were suffering in Llar. One day she said to me: 'Some people say that there are lots of things in Opus Dei, but I can see the lack of bare necessities in this house....'

"She finished off with a comment which I liked a lot: 'If you want to know something, the first thing you have to do is practice it. Only then can you pass judgment.' "

A remarkable change

Her mother takes up the story again. "She changed remarkably from the time she began going to Llar. Her brothers and sisters noticed it too. They used to tease her about being fat, just to annoy her, and she would get cross.... But from then on she gradually became more even tempered. She did not respond, and her brothers stopped teasing her. They realized they were wasting their time....

"She also began correcting some character defects gradually. For instance, she hated being called Montsita. But she never protested. And when someone in Llar would call her Montsita not knowing that it bothered her, she would just smile silently.

I also observed how she began to fulfill a simple spiritual plan of life. She would struggle to leap out of bed as soon as she awoke, not yielding to laziness.... She would fly off to school. At lunch time she would come home, eat frugally, and off she would go again to class. From school she would go to Llar. She did her homework there and a short period of mental prayer. She would attend a formation class of one kind or another and she would help with the running of the Center; in fact, she took care of everything referring to the oratory, something she loved to do. Some weekends she would go on an excursion."

"In fact, Montse had a wonderful time in Llar," Pepa concludes. "Indeed," remarks her mother smiling, "she had such a good time in Llar that she often came home quite late. I went there one day to complain and ask them to push her to come home earlier...!"

Not a minute to spare

Rosa goes on. "Her best friends were Ana María Suriol, Sylvia Pons, and others of her age." Nevertheless we got along very well even though I was a few years older. We used to talk about everything: films, theater, apostolic plans with mutual friends. We were starting Opus Dei activities with young people in Barcelona and we did not have a second to lose....

"One day I remember we were talking about God. I was saying that fulfilling God's will was the only important thing in our life. What would my life be without God? 'Look, Montse, I said, not realizing the implication of what I was saying. 'At the moment you are healthy, but at a given moment your health can fail as mine did. And then? Your life will fall apart if you are not close to God.'

'You are absolutely right, Rosa,' she answered, 'I want to be close to God too. If what happened to you should one day happen to me, I would like to maintain the same happiness and the same *joie de vivre* I have now....' On one occasion she said to me, 'Look what I am planning to do: to mortify my sight. I like to see everything. Walking along the street I look around everywhere. When I am passing a bookshop, or a boutique, I like to look... and in the talks they have said that I must begin to mortify myself in these little things.'

'Those things don't bother me. I prefer to read or listen to music...,' I said.

'Of course. So not looking for you wouldn't be the same mortification as for me.'

'Too true,' I thought. 'Montse is right. She generally walks along the streets and because of my situation I never do. So it must be more difficult for someone who walks past them often.'

"A week later she told me she had been struggling to live these small mortifications and was succeeding in not looking at lots of things...."

Montse was taking her first steps on the road to mortification done for love of God. Little mortifications in sight. Curiosity. "Haven't you ever opposed your whims and desires?" the founder of Opus Dei inquires. "The one who asks is nailed to a cross, suffering in all his senses and faculties, with a crown of thorns on his head... for you."

"However, we did not spend all day talking about spiritual things," Rosa continues. We played practical jokes on each other and told funny stories...we shared many intimate confidences. I remember I used to invite her to come to the meditation the priest gave every Saturday; sometimes she would say: 'You're overdoing it. Don't nag.'

"However, she always came in the end.

"We had the meditations in the oratory in Llar. There was a bare wooden cross on one wall of the oratory. A few times I said, encouraging her to be generous:

'Look at the cross, Montse. This is your cross. You can pick it up whenever you like...'

"She would answer 'Rosa, you go on and on about the cross.'

"And I would say 'keep looking at it....' "

3

Freedom and Joy

In Seva once more

In 1955 Manuel's working situation got back
to normal with a new job in a building firm. At the
end of the school year the Grases returned to Seva as
usual. This was where Montse had recovered from
her illness several years earlier.

At that time, Seva was a small town of about
one thousand inhabitants in the district of Osona,
situated 2,000 feet above sea level, south of the
Montseny mountain range. To those who were fed
up with city noise and pollution, it offered clean
skies, quiet village life, and a delightful cool breeze
in the evenings. The Grases rented 'Villa Josefa,' a
large elegant house in the village.

"We did our best to live those summer months
in a Christian fashion, and we tried to keep the
children busy. We tried to avoid those periods of
useless spare time 'with our senses awake and our

soul asleep,' which is the great danger of holidays. We encouraged them to read, to play sports, to make new friends...."

María Luisa Xiol, one of Montse's best friends, says: "We were never idle. When we were not out and about, we would stay at home and play cards or read.... Montse loved to sing, swim, cycle, and play tennis, or table tennis.... I remember her having a great love for sports and a great love for life... A lively girl."

Some Sundays Manuel and Manolita would go on an excursion to Montseny with some of their children and their friends. They would set off very early in the morning carrying their knapsacks, have lunch by a stream or seek the shelter of a farmhouse in the rain, and return through one of the mountain villages; Viladrau, Tagamanent, El Figaró, Aigua-freda, or San Marçal....

María Luisa wistfully evokes those days: "I remember the September evenings with the days getting shorter, coming down the Brull road singing our heads off on the way home from excursions with the moon and the stars shining. We would visit the Blessed Sacrament in the church at Brull."

One particular day the conversation between them became more intimate, more personal. María Luisa relates: "It happened one evening coming down from Agudes. Montse had not climbed to the top because her parents considered it to be too dangerous. On the way back, they came to fetch us. Darkness fell and all the while Montse and I, who had become separated from the main group, were talking about Jesus Christ: how, when we were sad, we should go to him – Montse called him 'Our Lord' – and how much it helped to rely on him."

The children of the vacationers formed a big group of friends. Montse was part of it and fitted in very well. She did not like cliques, those exclusive friendships that always destroy the big clan feeling. "She was at ease in any group," María Luisa recalls. She had that rare knack for getting along with people, of knowing when to talk and when to be silent.

Keeping quiet was a little mortification, which must have been hard at times, because she was very open by nature and always acted with great naturalness.

The boys and girls in the group knew perfectly well the limits of her naturalness. They knew she would not stand for certain jokes or for taking certain liberties... if not let them ask Andres Framis who, for a joke, took her headscarf home with him and... next day had to contend with the hot temper of the eldest Grases girl! María Luisa Xiol says: "At first she was a bit sensitive and things done, even without evil intent, upset her. However, she quickly forgot them again."

These events did not leave Andres any the worse for the wear. Besides, he was a good, fine, friendly lad, "a trustworthy man," according to the mothers who were always relieved when he went along on the excursions. Montse got along with him as well as with everyone else... providing, of course, that he returned her headscarf forthwith!

María Luisa relates the plans they made: "Montse was not a flirt or at all complicated in her dealings with boys. I don't think, at least she never told me, she ever fell in love; nor did she have a particular preference for one...."

Dancing sardanas

Now and again life in Seva relinquished its habitual monotony. There would be a commotion in the market square, where locals and vacationers would congregate . From house to house the news spread like wildfire: "Run, run, La Cobla has arrived and they are dancing sardanas in the square."

Sardanas. One could not conceive of a fiesta in Catalonia without this traditional dance. What a joy to lift up one's hands in the circle all together: fathers, mothers, neighbors, friends, all bound together in the slow rhythmic music. Such an elegant, joyful, ceremonious rhythm, just like the spirit of Catalonia herself...! How right Joan Maragall was when he sang *The Sardana*:

> *Of all the dances that were ever invented,*
> *the Sardana is the most beautiful.*
> *It is a magnificent moving ring*
> *which moves to a slow swaying measure.*
> *It is the sincere dance of a people who*
> *love each other and go forward with clasped*
hands!

As a good Catalan, Montse liked to dance the sardana, and she danced very well. Her friends remember her dancing the sardana on the big feasts of the surrounding villages. Her mother says: "Every time I hear the sardana I am reminded of you, Montsina... The truth is the sardana is like you, joyful and solemn. It is beautiful and one can look heavenward while doing it!"

The first pair of long trousers

Manolita recalls: "Over Christmas that year Fr. Gabriel, a diocesan priest who was Enrique's spiritual director, offered to say Mass for the whole family in the oratory of a house on Modolell Street in Barcelona. It was the occasion when Enrique got his first pair of long trousers.

"I realize that nowadays this business of the 'first pair of long trousers' means nothing. But it did then. It was a coming of age in a certain sense. And we wanted to celebrate it because it was a golden opportunity to have another family party at Christmas time.

"Everyone in the family took part in the preparations. Montse had the task of buying flowers for the altar. However, we realized later on, that as the afternoon went by she started to feel ill although she did not tell us about it so as not to spoil the party.

"When she was about to arrange the flowers she felt worse and left them there. She took a trolleycar to Llar and sat there until she felt a little better. Then she came home and tried to carry on as if nothing were the matter. However, we realized at once how ill she was; she looked really awful.

"Next day was Christmas Eve and she had to go to bed. We took her to the doctor and he found her anemic. After several more visits, they discovered two weeks later that she had an abscess in the lower half of the duodenum. The doctor recommended total bed rest, and so she spent two weeks in bed. A long convalescence followed. This was why she did not play although she had just been picked for the basketball team of the Tennis Club in Barcino. We spent the following summer, 1956 in Calella, but she could hardly swim."

How wonderful it was in Calella!

Calella was – before the boom of the sixties – a small town on the Catalonian coast. The Grases spent some weeks there in the summer of 1956. They swapped houses with another family who had a convalescent child who needed the Montseny air of Seva.

Calella had neither the peak of Matagalla, or the Montseny air, or the peacefulness of Villa Josefa, but it did have a fabulous beach. Laughing and shouting the young Grases spent the day – and part of the night if they were allowed – jumping about among the waves. There were nine of them now. Rafael, another boy, was born on February 8 that year.

How wonderful it was in Calella! The hours flew by, with one dip after another, splashing about among heads and floats. Then suddenly they came down to earth for lunch, which meant the end of bathing and the arrival of the egg and sand sandwich, or sand and egg in the worst of cases, followed by a get-together under the sunshade.

Manuel Grases makes the comment: "At that time there was generally nothing on the beach that offended Christian sensibilities. If it were otherwise, we would not have been there; as Christian parents there is no point in offering one's children an occasion of offending God with the false excuse of having a holiday. Those days on the beach had just one drawback – they came to an end!"

Montse was convalescent still, so she had to watch her brothers and sisters play in the water... from the beach. "She had a very pretty swimsuit that was decorous," her father comments. She was modest with complete naturalness, never looking for attention.

Although, if truth were known, she did not care if she did attract attention in the little details of decency. She was not inhibited by what others thought of her. "She was clean of heart and she had great purity," María Luisa comments.

❀   ❀   ❀

Montse had understood the profound meaning of Christian naturalness, which can be interpreted as not being "one of the crowd." When she had to go against the grain, she knew how to carry out that point (380) of *The Way* in her own life: "'And in a pagan or in a worldly atmosphere, when my life clashes with its surroundings won't my naturalness seem artificial?' you asked me. And I reply: 'Undoubtedly your life will clash with theirs; and that contrast – because you are confirming your faith with works – is exactly the naturalness I ask of you.'"

Montse never lived in a "pagan or worldly" environment, though she did live in an atmosphere then, as now, of "human respect" or concern about the opinions of others. In that climate she lived out her Christianity as the founder of Opus Dei asked, spontaneously, without doing odd things or behaving in a holier-than-thou way. And let us not camouflage what is really an offense against God, a sin, with the false excuse of "naturalness." Both at home and in Llar she had learned to protect the virtue of holy purity by setting up the struggle far from the fortress: in those small details of decency and modesty which protect it. She practiced this virtue decisively and simply. The virtue of simplicity was evident in all her actions. Her mother tells: "When they used to ask me, some time ago now, what Montse was like when she was young, 'Could you see already she was extraordinary? ' I would reply: 'No!' Because I did not know what they were referring to.

"Now I would say 'yes'. Because what is extraordinary is precisely that of being clear, simple, transparent, and ingenuous. That is how she was throughout her life. I remember one girl who as soon as a lad came near her, left Montse in an uncomfortable situation. She turned her back on her as if she did not know her. She did this as often as the occasion demanded.

"One day Montse came home practically in tears saying, "I don't know why she does that to me, Mom." She did not understand her. She had no conception of someone being two-faced. Was it worthwhile explaining it to her? I think not. So I said, 'Look here, that is how she is.'

"There was no protest or criticism of her behavior, only silence."

Silence. Perhaps silence is one of the most eloquent things in Montse's life, especially at the moment of obeying. "She was very obedient," María Luisa says. Those silences, especially if one is right, reveal great humility and a strong human personality and were made manifest in very different situations. For instance, that August night in Seva...

Manolita says, "She had gone on an excursion with some others. It got very late at night and they were not back... All of the families were very worried; and when they finally came I punished her. As I thought it was a serious lack of responsibility, I said there would be no more excursions alone with her friends.

"When I think of it now I almost faint, above all because the blame for the delay was not hers. However, her reaction was laudable. She never answered me back, never showed disrespect or impudence. When something hurt her like what I have just described, the only thing she did was become very serious, lower her eyes, and nothing else. And that is what she did..."

And then, one day

"And then, one day that summer, when we least expected it, Enrique told us he wanted to be a priest...," Manolita recalls.

"It was a surprise. We were delighted because we had always asked God to give vocations to our children. However, like this, so sudden, just sixteen years of age, having just finished the fifth year of the "Bachillerato" ...indeed we were surprised. No, we had not been expecting it."

Manuel takes up the story. "We went to see Fr. Gabriel then, his spiritual director. Fr. Gabriel advised us to let him act freely. With great emphasis he told us that if he were in our shoes, he would take great care not to put our son's vocation in jeopardy by using delay tactics.

"From a human point of view the separation was very hard. However, we thought it over in the presence of God and we saw that really it was not a sacrifice but – as the founder of Opus Dei teaches – a sign of divine predilection for our family. This was

what I had been praying for since God gave him to
me, and now he was granting me my request... So I
said to Enrique: 'Look, this is my advice to you.
This year you should switch from studying the
Sciences to the Humanities and do sixth year
humanities. Then as soon as you finish the
secondary school you can go to the seminary. If not,
you will find Latin and Greek very hard to pick up
when you get there. What do you think about getting
some private tutoring in Greek now, during the
summer, so it does not catch you quite by surprise?
Think about it, and let me know what you decide.'"

Manolita concludes the story: "That same
summer, on our Lady's feast day, August 15,
Enrique wrote a letter to his father who was away
for a few days, saying how he had prayed to our
Lady and had commended his vocation into her
hands; how thanks to her he had seen clearly what
he should do: when he finished sixth year, he would
enter the seminary."

His parents knew. Now he would have to tell
his brothers and sisters.

"Next year I am going into the seminary," he
said one evening suddenly over dinner. "I am going
to be a priest."

Montse and Jorge were astonished. "What did
you say, Enrique? You're going to be..."

"Yes, that is what I said. I am going to be a
priest."

     ❀   ❀   ❀

This is rather like what happens in photo-graphy, when the foreground is sharply focused and the background is blurred. We have no intimation of the repercussion in Montse's soul of her big brother's generous self-giving to God in the full flush of youth. Ana María Suriol assures us that "it was 'one of the greatest joys Montse had in her life...' When Montse told me the news, her eyes filled with tears of joy and she gave me a big hug. She spoke lovingly of her brother and at the same time with great respect and admiration." From then on the attention in the Grases household centered on the boy who would very soon be leaving for the seminary. Montse was left behind, in the back-ground.

Enrique recalls: "We never spoke of my vocation, just as I never asked her what she did in the Center of Opus Dei. We never spoke of these things."

However, even though we do not have written testimonies, it is highly probable that her brother's self-giving to God as a priest, a brother who was very close to her, should evoke ideals of self-giving and love of God in her. It must have left a profound impression in the intimacy of her soul, possibly a decisive one on her road to sanctity.

But only God knows its full extent.

4

God whispers

At the professional school for women

Time passes relentlessly. Manolita's friends were saying: "Your daughter is a woman already." It was true. That October of 1956 Montse was fifteen. She had done her secondary schooling, the "Bachillerato". She was a beautiful girl, notable for her deep, penetrating eyes.

"She wanted to be a nurse," her mother says, "but she was two years too young to register in nursing school; so we advised her to register in a special municipal school in the meantime, where she would learn things that would come in useful in the future." So she had to leave her old school. "She found it hard, but registered in the new school without any complaint," her father said.

Her friend Ana María Suriol also wanted to become a nurse. And her parents prudently advised her to do some voluntary work before beginning her studies. "That is what we did," Ana María Suriol recalls. "We went to St Paul's Hospital for a few months. We began practically as junior nurses; we learnt a few things; but Montse was not exactly happy in the wards. She treated the patients very lovingly, but she was fearful and apprehensive, not daring to do some things like giving injections."

The professional school for women – *L'Escola* as it was popularly known – is situated in the very heart of Barcelona, near the Cathedral. It is a prestigious academic center. Montse signed up for Domestic Science, Drawing, Sewing and Crafts. She learned a lot in that school as she had great manual abilities, which could be seen in her admission test.

However, her mother says: "Although *L'Escola* was pretty good, it was clearly not Montse's environment. Nearly all the students were much older than she was, with all the differences that brings – more frivolity, unsuitable conversations etc – as well as having a drawing teacher who played unkind jokes on her and told her she was too serious.…"

Her study of the piano was not particularly interesting either, in spite of her good marks and her love for music. However, she obeyed and continued with her lessons.

The first retreat

Throughout that year Montse attended talks and meditations at Llar. They encouraged her to sanctify her work, to do it in God's presence. It was not just a case of passing all the subjects in June, but of meeting our Lord in class in *L'Escola*, offering up work well done, trying to do it as perfectly as possible.

She went to Mass often. On Sunday mornings after Mass she was always ready to play tennis with her old racquet . She had breakfast, met up with one of her friends, and off to Barcino! Later on, they would come home together commenting on their game.

"You were lucky today, Montse, one more and you would not have won. If it weren't for that serve...."

"What about the half-volley of mine? What do you say about that?"

"You were lucky. You caught me unawares...."

And among these comments Montse would extend an invitation to her friend, which would catch her even more off guard:

"Listen, why don't you come to Llar? Do you know we have a meditation on Saturdays?"

❀   ❀   ❀

Every good player knows the rule. You have to be prepared, with your own tactics, for your opponent to attack you when you least expect it.

She, who would invite her friends, found herself one day fending off an invitation as best she could....

"One day after a piano lesson," Rosa recalls, "I invited her to a retreat. She answered:

'I will go whenever I want to, not when you tell me.'

"I have to admit that her reply surprised me a bit. In fact I did not like it at all. For two reasons: First of all because I really wanted her to go on that retreat; and secondly, because we were good friends and it was the first thing of this type I had suggested to her. Nor was I asking for such a big thing!

"But she did not go. She went later on, just like she said, to the retreat she wanted to go on. However, even though I did not like her answer, I respected her freedom, because in Opus Dei I had been taught to love the freedom of others, not to be heavy-handed with anyone, least of all in spiritual matters.

"Montse would never allow herself to be dominated by anybody, not for a minute... She had her own ideas. And even though she took no notice of me; this was what I liked about her. At fifteen she had tremendous personality. She was not a weak person, not by any means. Anybody can manipulate weak personalities. No, Montse was not to be manipulated!"

Castelldaura

But she did go on a retreat at the end of

November in Castelldaura, a new Conference Center of Opus Dei in Barcelona.

"It was the first retreat we had organized in Castelldaura," recalls Carmiña Cameselle, a member of Opus Dei who lived in Llar. "The house had just been bought and lots of things needed to be done. Montse was very apostolic and she brought two friends with her."

Pepa adds: "That retreat followed the usual pattern: a meditation given by the priest in the morning, Holy Mass, a visit to the Blessed Sacrament at midday, saying the rosary, the Stations of the Cross...."

It was an intense spiritual exercise, which the attendants adapted to their own way of life, proper to their age. "Montse was very naughty," Carmiña recalls, "and the night they arrived made a lot of noise and came down the stairs roaring with laughter and making a terrible racket. At the bottom of the stairs they met the director who reprimanded them. As Montse was quick tempered, she got cross...."

She got over her bad temper pretty quickly. Next day with the help of the meditations she began to focus deeply into her relationship with our Lord. The priest who gave the retreat "gave very fine meditations that moved us to the love of God." Rosa continues: "After some of these talks she came and whispered – it was a silent retreat – 'Rosa, today I am going to have lots to think about.'"

Have you ever thought that....

"That first retreat meant a strong spiritual impulse to Montse," Rosa comments, "although she already had formed habits of interior life because there was a deeply pious environment in her home. They prayed and learned to love God as a Father and our Lady as a Mother with complete naturalness. For instance, the first thing Montse did when she arrived home every day was to greet Our Lady of Montserrat, whose image was at the end of the corridor. Thus many of the customs of Christian living that they taught her in Opus Dei, she was living already. She had learned them at home."

"One day she quizzed me about my vocation to Opus Dei. I told her it was something very personal. 'But you have to tell me,' she insisted. So I told her, and we began to talk about vocation in general. 'How happy you are,' she said.

'Well, you could be equally happy if God gave you a vocation to the Work.'

'And how do I know if I have a vocation?'

'You discover your vocation in prayer," I replied, "because it is God who gives us our vocation. It is neither people nor friends who give it. You have to discover it for yourself...'

"She did not know yet that her parents were in Opus Dei, as they had not told her, to respect her freedom, though she did know they went to the means of spiritual formation of Opus Dei. Then I seized the opportunity and I inquired more specifically:

'Montse, has it never occurred to you to think that God could call you to Opus Dei? Why don't you think about it?'"

"And why should I think about it?"

The retreat finished. "One day I noticed Montse was very worried," her mother recalls. "So I asked her what the matter was. She told me everything because she trusted me.

'Mom, they said "Think. Has it never occurred to you...?" Tell me: why should I think about it?'

"I found her surprised and disconcerted. I told her not worry but to take it easy. However she continued to be worried. She did not see it. 'Me? in Opus Dei...?' she said to herself over and over. She decided to stop going to Llar.

"The next day I went to Llar and spoke to the director. We agreed that the best thing was for no one to call her. If she wanted to go, fine; but if not no one was to insist.

"For a few days she did not appear in the Center. However, after a few days with no one's bidding, she went back...

"I must say, I was very glad she went back, as I hoped God would grant her a vocation... I had prayed a lot for this intention, and I put all the means at my disposal to help her to be generous. But I always left her free, as I had been taught in Opus

Dei that without freedom one cannot love God...."

The freedom that Montse enjoyed is made manifest in numerous details. Her parents were in Opus Dei but they did not force her – following a lively recommendation of the founder – to carry out any type of devotion, much less to attend any Center of Opus Dei. She always went to Llar because she wanted to. The fact that she went there did not mean she lost contact with her friends from the Dominicans.

❧   ❧   ❧

You cannot love God without freedom... or without cheerfulness. Fortunately Montse enjoyed both these in abundance. Cheerfulness was one of the features of the environment in Llar that most attracted her.

Sometimes she would go with her brother Enrique and a whole gang of friends to the concerts at the Music Palace. Only the older children went there. "I used to plead with them to take me," Jorge, her younger brother, recalls. "I would say I liked music too, but not a chance. They would never take me. Not even once."

Other Sunday mornings Montse would go with her friends to dance sardanas at the Virtelia School or in one of the city squares. Pepa recalls: "At that time this was the custom in Barcelona.

Every Sunday it would be in a different place; young girls would arrange to meet there to watch or to participate. Montse loved to go, as much to listen to the music as to go for a walk."

One of the favorite places for young people to congregate at that time was Paseo de Gracia, a wide boulevard between Consejo de Ciento and the Diagonal. They would walk up and down, in groups, according to their ages, or form impromptu get-togethers sitting in a circle on rented chairs, which cost just a few cents apiece.

The walks she did with Rosa were rather special because of her physical condition. Generally this meant doing a bit of a tour, dodging among the noisy buses, in a specially adapted Isetta, a tiny single-cylinder German car. The tour would end in the Catalonian Square where they would stop for a while under the Italian mountain oaks to enjoy the hustle and bustle of people coming and going among the pigeons, or sitting talking on the rows of wooden chairs arranged concentrically around the fountain. Later on they would go up the Catalonian Avenue and inevitably end up in Lezo, a cafe that was user-friendly from Rosa's point of view: It had no steps, it had a large deep, comfortable seat all along the wall, and it was a fashionable place. What more could one want?

At other times they would stay at home and listen to music. Rosa assures us that "she just adored rancheras. Especially those Mexican songs sung by Jorge Negrete, which she would join in with all her might:

> *When a Mexican loves*
> *His love is like no other*
> *His self-giving is beyond*
> *Compare, and with no conditions."*

Montse could not imagine then how these words would become reality in her own life which, from that moment onwards, would take a complete turn.

The second retreat

In October, just after the holidays, Enrique entered the diocesan seminary of Barcelona. Montse had been to France on a short student exchange and now she returned to *L'Escola* to continue her classes. Her good marks were evidence of the formation she was receiving in Llar about sanctifying work: She got mostly A's and B's.

She kept going to Llar frequently. In November 1957 Rosa invited her again to go on retreat. "I said I did not know if I would be able to go on this retreat....

'Why?' she inquired.

'Because a friend of mine was coming to help me, and now she can't. The fact is if no one comes who can help me, I can't see myself going alone. I don't like everybody to have to be at my beck and call.'

'Okay,' she said to me at once, 'then I will go

and help you.'

"This was a typical gesture of hers, to help as much as she could. And she did it very elegantly, not calling attention to herself. She would help and then disappear without leaving one abandoned; suddenly you would turn around and there she would be ready to help again...

"This attitude can become second nature in an adult, but in a young girl like her it was surprising. She was attentive to the big things and the little ones. If I noticed she would wink at me, smiling, as if saying, 'it's all taken care of !'

"Anyway, for different reasons, I did not go on this retreat. I stayed in Barcelona and prayed a lot for her – because I was convinced she had a vocation. It was clear that Montse had a spirit of detachment, she was generous and appeared to have a capacity for self-giving. And her heart was free to love God...

"One day I said so to her very clearly:

'Look Montse, God has given you certain qualities and I am convinced that if you give yourself to God, you will be very happy. Why don't you ask our Lord if you have a vocation?'

"I am quite sure that she, too, had figured this out. But she did not like to hear me say it. She answered that vocation was something very important, and very personal; but that she had to decide in total freedom.

"And, of course, I left her in total freedom. But I continued to pray for her vocation..."

Lía Vila

A new director came to Llar on November 5; her name was Emilia Vila. However, we all called her by her nickname, Lía. Montse's mother remembers a Catalan woman of twenty-seven, originally from the city of Gerona, a woman of great qualities and extremely friendly. "She was tall and thin with chestnut hair. She was dynamic and had apostolic zeal, with an open, extroverted temperament. She was cheerful and serene at the same time."

When Lía came to Llar, Pepa Castelló introduced her to some of the young girls who came to the Center. One of them was shrouded in a white coat and was helping to fix things in the house, actually cleaning paint off a door. When she saw Lía she went forward to greet her:

"Hello. My name is Montse. What is yours?"

In her recollections Lía recalls: "Montse struck me very specially." Soon after this brief encounter she had a chance to spend some days with Montse in Castelldaura during the retreat.

Montse had gone on retreat with her friend Ana María Suriol. They were the two youngest of the twelve who were on retreat, and they found it very hard to keep the silence. "The two of them talked a lot," Lía says amused, "but we did not say anything to them." Lía and Pepa understood how, at their age, after the talks and meditations by the priest, they just wanted to chat and take a walk, giggling, around the garden....

They discovered the reason for all the giggles later on. The very first day, as soon as they arrived at Castelldaura, Montse had tried all the beds in the house, one by one, to see which was the softest, most comfortable one. When she decided which was the best, she leapt on it as if on the top of a trampoline, until... crack! To the consternation of Ana María who was looking on, both bed and Montse collapsed to the floor. They tied the bed up with rope. What a way to begin a retreat!, they thought.

Anyway, Lía and Pepa encouraged the two young chatterboxes to take full advantage of the retreat to deepen their dealings with God, and to strive to keep silence because God speaks in whispers....

It was only a murmur, as God really whispers. Montse felt instinctively, in the depths of her heart, what God wanted of her... though not completely. As often happens when God calls, she had to overcome some small doubt.

Apparently nothing had happened. Nobody noticed. Not even Ana María. All she noticed was a greater happiness in Montse. She says: "Those days we intensified our spiritual conversations. However, she did not tell me about her vocation or about her desire to give herself to our Lord until some time later, when she saw God's call more clearly."

Lía Vila recalls how from the retreat onwards they would talk together about some aspects of the interior life, more particularly prayer. For spiritual reading Lía recommended *Man the Saint,* a book by

Jesus Urteaga, which Montse loved, and *Mary of Nazareth,* by Federico Suarez, which she took to heart. They were really decisive in her life....

About that time, December 8, Sylvia Pons had decided to give herself to God in Opus Dei. Montse was not surprised. She had commented during the retreat to Nuria, a friend of hers, that you could see it coming...

Sylvia's generous decision must have been a bugle call to her soul just as her brother, Enrique's, had been. Sylvia was Montse's age more or less and here she was already committed....

María del Carmen Delclaux recalls, "Sylvia was a pretty girl, from a very good Barcelona family. She was very dynamic and, for that time, very independent. She drove an Isetta and enjoyed great freedom of movement, which was not at all common then. I remember she used to pick us up in her car and take us here and there. The fact that she had so much autonomy surprised us, for girls, at least in Barcelona, used to live very sheltered lives with their families."

Doubts and fears

Montse, like Sylvia, enjoyed an atmosphere of freedom in her family, and the two got along extremely well due to her open, friendly, independent disposition. Montse also felt the call of God in the depths of her soul: it would float to the surface every time she did the prayer... Point 903 of *The*

Way was like a sharp sword: "If you see your way clearly, follow it. Why don't you shake off the cowardice that holds you back?"

It became more and more obvious... yes, that was what God was asking her for... this was it... but, she thought, I am so young, it is too soon... Am I not going too fast ?

❀   ❀   ❀

"Mom, I think I have a vocation."

When Manolita heard these words from her daughter's lips she was disconcerted. She had always dreamt of having a son become a priest, and there Enrique was... Deep down she had always wished that her children would give themselves to God, and now Montse was telling her....

However, she had thought, without knowing why, that this would happen years ahead, way in the future, as if time stood still....

Maybe, like all mothers, she had not realized that her "children" were no longer children and that the moment she had prayed for was here, so soon!

"But Montse, have you thought about it properly?"

"Yes, Mom. Yes, I have. I have a vocation, and I want to ask for admission as a numerary."

What could she say? Montse was looking at her, awaiting her reply. What reply could she give her? There is nothing more fragile than a vocation born in a young soul. What should she do? Tell her to wait a bit like Enrique? Fr. Gabriel had said that young people should not be asked to put off their self-giving; that when God calls, the answer has to be yes; that parents put their souls in danger when they place serious obstacles in the way of their children's vocation.

But it could be just an illusion, a juvenile whim, which goes away as soon as it comes. But what if it were God's doing? How could she oppose something if it were from God.

"Montse, have you talked it over with your spiritual director?"

"No, Mom. I want to be sure first."

"Well I think you should, because he can help you. Shall we tell Dad?"

Montse was not enthusiastic. Manolita insisted. Montse hesitated for a few more seconds. She had not counted on that. She gave in: "Okay, let's tell him."

Manuel Grases heard the news with his customary aplomb. He tried to hide his delight.

"Look, Montse," he said in a calm voice, "all I can say to you is this: a vocation is the greatest gift God can bestow on us and presupposes a decision on your part, which you have to think through, in the presence of God. The only thing your mother and I can do in this case is to pray and, since it is Christmastide, what the three of us should do is commend it to the Child Jesus, so that he makes you see your vocation clearly. What do you say?"

Manuel Grases contained himself as best he could. Indeed this was what he had been praying for all his life... God was giving him, exactly as he had been asking, another vocation among his children. But what mattered now was not his own delight but fulfilling God's will.

And they set themselves to pray.

❀   ❀   ❀

Manuel and Manolita Grases acted like good Christian parents: they left their daughter in total freedom to decide for herself before God. They had not told her that they themselves already belonged to Opus Dei, not because there was a lack of trust or a silly secret. It was rather a delicate sign of consideration for her; they thought that this gave her greater freedom in her decision.

Neither did they tell her they had been praying for her to give herself to God some day. They did not resolve her doubt but they gave her the best way to clear it up, which was to discuss her decision with experienced people. And they let her decide for herself, in total freedom, face to face with God.

On their side, they used the supernatural means to know God's will: they trusted to prayer.

❀   ❀   ❀

On December 22, at 11 a.m. in the morning, Radio Vatican broadcast the Pope's Christmas message to the whole world. You could hear the deep solemn voice of Pius XII over the airwaves: "God has entrusted his designs to people to carry them out personally and freely, with complete moral responsibility, and demanding if necessary, fatigue and sacrifices in Christ's service."

❧   ❧   ❧

Pepa and Montse had a long conversation on the afternoon of Christmas Eve. Pepa recalls: "Montse came to help me finish setting up the Crib. Then we went out together to do some last minute shopping. We went as far as the cathedral square, where the open market was, where you could buy Crib figures, tambourines, moss…. We were talking about her vocation and she told me her leg was aching; but I did not take much notice. She had almost decided to join Opus Dei, but she was held back by the fear of not persevering.

Montse expressed her doubts: Maybe she was too young…. Pepa told her about Icíar, the director of a Center of Opus Dei in Rome, who had decided to join the Work at her age. Montse countered: Who would reassure her about the future…? Who could assure her of perseverance? And what if she were not strong enough? Pepa gave her supernatural reasons until, at a particular moment, Montse abandoned herself into God's hands and decided. There was nothing more to say: God was calling her to Opus Dei.

She returned to Llar absolutely overjoyed. She was completely decided now. And happy, although a bit nervous.

María del Carmen Delclaux says: "I remember perfectly. It was 8 p.m. and I was with Montse ironing the altar linen. She was uneasy, coming and going from the room where we were ironing to the door of Lía's office, which was busy then. She told me she was waiting to be able to talk to her. I was surprised by her uneasiness. Then she said: "Later on, will you show me how to iron the altar linen?" I was puzzled. What could she mean by saying "later on"?

At last, the door of Lía's office opened and Montse ran towards it: "Lía, can I speak to you for a moment?"

The first letter

Lía concludes: "No, it was not a sentimental, momentary rapture; or a whim of the moment. Montse was a stable girl. She did not act on sudden impulse. I knew her well. It was a mature, meditated decision, and totally free. It was not the result of any external influence: Montse had a strong personality, not easily influenced. It was from God."

Lía had thought over Montse's vocation for a

long time and considered it in God's presence. After talking to Montse she was convinced of the spiritual maturity of her young soul and her sincere desire for self-giving and struggle. She knew she wished to ask for admission to Opus Dei, to serve the Church, to sanctify her daily work, to struggle for love's sake right up to the last minute.... And she let her ask for admission with a handwritten letter to the founder, in the friendly tone proper to the Work.

Montse took the pen into her hand nervously. This was surely the decisive, without doubt the most decisive, moment of her whole life. But she was quite decided: it was what God was asking her. She began to write.

Barcelona, December 25, 1957
Father,
My name is Montse Grases. I am still very young, but in spite of everything I have been coming to Llar for a long time and I have gotten to know the Work gradually and in the end I have come to love it. I made a retreat recently in Castelldaura, and it was decisive for me.

Then she asked for admission as a numerary in Opus Dei.

Although this was just a first step – it was only asking for admission in Opus Dei – even though there was no legal commitment whatsoever, nor would there be one until a few years had passed,

there she was with her soul committed to God in the
Work. She was already Opus Dei in her heart. What
a joy! She had committed herself to God on Christmas Eve!

That night, on her way home, everything
seemed much more beautiful: little Adriano Square,
the banana trees on the way down Muntaner Street,
which was also the route of the famous number 64
tram, the houses with big balconies from which you
could see, if you looked up the street between the
trees, as far as the peak of Tibidabo, and which were
lost if you looked down the street towards the port...
What a pity you could not see the sea from here!
Indeed, that Christmas everything was more beautiful: the pale street lamps, the shop windows all lit up
with Cribs and decorations... This was the happiest
Christmas of her life. Christmas, when Christ gives
himself to us for love, she had given herself freely
also for love – of God.

There was a celebration at home too. She was
dying to tell her parents everything.

"Well," they replied, "we belong to Opus Dei
too."

"What...? You... too? What luck! What
incredible luck!"

"She was bursting with joy," Manolita says,
"and with gratitude to God."

Then Manuel Grases proposed a toast for his
daughter... and the three of them began to sing
together:

The fields are ploughed
Love has opened the furrows
The world has become a path
for the wishes
of the sower...

They are so different

On the afternoon of the 25th there was a family get-together for those who had asked for admission to Opus Dei recently. Montse was there too, and according to Carmen Salgado who was Montse's age more or less, "she was overflowing with joy."

From that day on Lía recalls, Montse "continued with her normal life of study and work even though it was holiday time. She went to Mass early in the morning at Llar, then she spent some time studying. She went home and helped her mother with the housework....

The Grases would listen everyday, as was the custom in most Spanish families, to the *communiqué* on the radio at 2.30 p.m. That is what they continued to call the news program, a hold-over from the war years when the military communiqué was eagerly awaited.

However, the national news, then, had nothing significant. Neither had the international news. Only the weather forecast was exciting. Snow on the hills. Snow? Montse did not need to think twice about it. Now was the right time to go skiing!

"How excited she was about the excursion!" her mother recalls. "We went to a shop near Provenza Street where you could rent things, and then with her own sweaters as well, she was fully equipped. I got up early to see her off."

It is quite likely that she went to very early Mass, as was the custom with a lot of the Barcelona sports people. Later she took the famous "ski train," which went as far as the farthest point in the valley. There they put on their skis, firmly attached to their leather boots with straps...

The view was fabulous You could see the peaks of Puig-Llançada and Coll de Pal, 7,500 and 8,100 feet respectively.

"When she came back three or four days later," Manolita continues, "she told me that on the way home, in the train, the others would not believe that it was the first time she had put on a pair of skis... I kept asking her if she had had a good time and all she would say was:

'Fine, fine. But they are different! Mom they are so different!'

"I began to get worried as she did not say anything else and I started to think that maybe something had happened.

'Has something happened to you, Montse?'

'No, Mom. It is just that they are so different!'

'So different in what, Montse?'

"I insisted so much that in the end she told me everything.

'It's like this. I felt quite lonely... I didn't

know anyone and so when I was trying to put my skis on I spoke to some girls. They had their skis on already and off they went. I was left alone and I had to manage on my own.'..."

In that precise moment Montse perceived very clearly that there are two ways of living in the world: the selfish way and the other way, being generous and concerned for others, proper to Christians, which she had learned from her parents and from Opus Dei. Two ways of living in the middle of the world. Totally different from each other!

Lía recalls: "She came back very happy but a bit worried as she had spent a lot, although she had tried to live the virtue of poverty pretty carefully. She had fulfilled her spiritual plan of life fairly well although in a slightly disorderly way. She said: 'It really wasn't easy.'"

"Shortly after coming back from the ski trip to La Molina we came out of Llar running, as we often did, down Muntaner Street," Sylvia recounts. "We were going home. Suddenly Montse stopped with an intense pain in her left leg: 'Oh! oh! oh!... Stop, please stop!' We stopped. And, I am ashamed to admit it, I said: 'Come on, don't exaggerate!' And we continued running down the hill to the corner of Travesera where we each went our different ways."

A funny Christmas gift

Many of the girls who lived in Llar had spent a few days away on retreat. When they got back to

Barcelona they discovered that Lía and the youngest ones had everything ready to celebrate. In Spain, the Three Kings take the place of Santa Claus, and they bring gifts on the Feast of the Epiphany, January 6. There was a fine throne set up in the living room, made from the sofa from the music room, covered over with colorful material and with several cushions as a footstool. Everything was ready to receive the important visitors with all the pomp and circumstance the bedspreads of the house could furnish! This time, Melchior, Casper, and Baltasar had delegated their jobs to Carmen Salgado, Ana María Suriol, and Montse Grases, who were received by the others with tremendous applause. There were small presents and joke gifts which hinted at a characteristic peculiar to each one, given out by their majesties, who had not forgotten their own presents. Montse got a little clay figure of a donkey and a needle-case in the shape of a painted red lamp.

Montse's characteristic was that if you asked her to sing to entertain the others, she sang. If it were necessary to dance, she danced. And if they asked her to be one of the Magi, she did it. She was not afraid of being a laughing-stock nor was she shy (often shyness is a kind of vanity and interior doubt: what will they think of me, how will I appear?...). She was incapable of duplicity. She would tell Lía with all sincerity what was going well and what was going badly in her efforts to incorporate the spirit of Opus Dei into her life. She relied on the grace of God. If she achieved the spiritual goals she was aiming at, she thanked God; if not she redoubled her efforts to improve. All of this, with simplicity, is the fruit of humility. Carmen Salgado recalls: "She would receive any corrections with serenity; she would listen attentively and then, smiling, would say 'Thank you.'"

❀   ❀   ❀

19 July 1941: The first ever photograph of Montse, taken on the day she was christened.

1945: A straightforward, spontaneous and vivacious child.

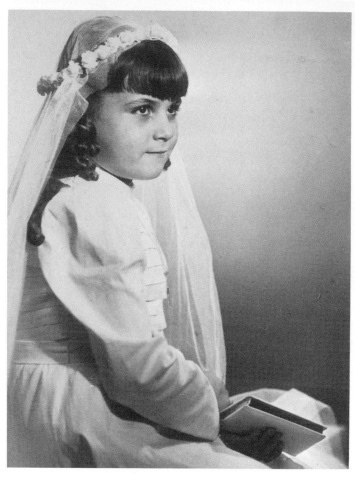

27 May 1945: Montse made her
First Holy Communion

"She had a cheerful and youthful attitude, always maintaining a balance of her own. I like the way she dressed," says Jorge Suriol.

"Whenever I hear a sardana I think of you, Montsina," her mother says. "It is because the sardana is like you, joyful and serious: it is pretty and one can look heavenwards while dancing it."

During the
summer
holidays.

1956: Playing
with two of her
younger brothers.

On a family pilgrimage to a shrine of our Lady on the outskirts of Barcelona.

Emilia (Lía) Vila was the Director of Llar, the Center of Opus Dei which Montse attended. Lía is an important witness to the holiness of the Servant of God.

At Castelldaura Conference Centre,
near Barcelona.

1958: With her father, Manuel

Montse is seen wearing a medal of Our Lady of
Montserrat which her mother had just given to her.
A family heirloom, it is decorated with precious
stones, and years earlier had been given by her
paternal grandmother to her mother.

June 1958: The whole of the Grases family

Montse with her brother, Enrique.

Montse with two of her friends, Javier Framis
and María Luisa.

Preparing to go
on stage in Seva.

After Sunday Mass, with her grandmother,
mother and her cousin, Angelines.

Rome, 13 November 1958: (*Left to right*) Don
Alvaro del Portillo, Blessed Josemaría Escrivá,
Iciar Zumalde, Montse and Encarnita Ortega.

November 1958: At a get-together in Rome

One of the last photographs taken, with her mother.

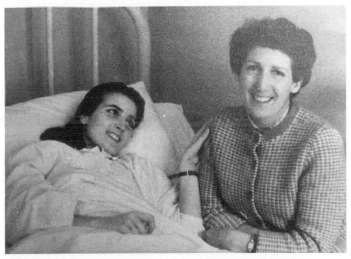

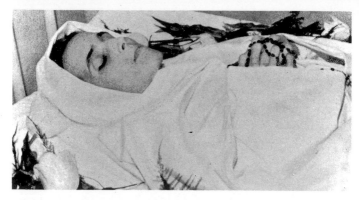

Her countenance has a serene and placid expression,
with a slight trace of a smile
and the imprint of her sufferings.

7 August 1989: Surrounded by their eight children
and thirteen grandchildren, Montse's parents
celebrated their golden wedding anniversary.
Here they are seen showing Pope John Paul II
the prayer card for private devotion to
the Servant of God, Montserrat Grases.

5

A fall in La Molina

One Sunday afternoon in January, Lía was surprised to see Montse limping. Her mother had also noticed it. Manolita says: "We called Dr. Sáenz, who came with his hearty and jovial manner as always, and he began by teasing her: 'Montse, why have you taken it into your head to get ill?'

"The doctor did not attach any importance to the pain in her knee and prescribed some vitamins. But the pain persisted. He saw her again soon and told her to wear a knee-guard. He was surprised by her physical decline and was really perplexed.

'What I cannot understand,' he said, 'is her looking like this, with the huge quantity of vitamins she is taking. That is what really worries me.'"

"Montse thought that the knee-guard she had been told to wear was going to be some kind of orthopedic apparatus," Carmen Salgado recalls. "When she told me about it in Llar, I told her I had one and could lend it to her. I showed it to her and as soon as she saw it she laughed, saying: 'For goodness sake, my brothers wear those to play hockey. I thought it was going to be something very expensive!' And she was pleased with herself for not having to put her parents to any expense."

It had been a simple fall. Maybe a nerve had got swollen and needed a bit of rest. But the pain continued and she limped a bit. Rosa recalls: "When I saw her coming towards me limping, I thought she was pulling my leg and I said, 'And on top of it all you make fun of those of us who walk like this.'

'No, I am not making fun of you at all. It is just that I fell and my knee hurts!'"

Montse thought the pain was due to one of the falls she had had at La Molina.

She'll be back!

"Don't you long to shout to those youths who are bustling around you: Fools! Leave those worldly things that shackle the heart and very often degrade it... Leave all that and come with us in search of Love!" (*The Way*, 790).

Montse did a period of prayer every day in front of the Blessed Sacrament, and points of *The Way*, like the one above, fired her with love of God and stirred her to have greater desires of apostolate and co-redemption. She knew that her vocation – the greatest grace our Lord had given her – urged her to sanctify her work and presupposed total commitment to the apostolate: "*You have not chosen me but I have chosen you that you may go out and bear fruit....*"

Bear fruit... How? Nobody knows anything when they are born; so she had to learn how to do apostolate gradually. It was not so hard to learn because the apostolate is not a technique; rather, in the words of the founder of Opus Dei, it is "an overflow of interior life." Montse did have interior life: she prayed, she was pious, she received our Lord in the Eucharist, she had an intimate relationship with the Sacred Humanity of Jesus Christ, she tried to deepen in her eucharistic devotion, she was growing in her desire to atone...; as well as this, she had lots of friends and knew how to love them. She offered up little mortifications for them and commended them to God in her prayer. Sylvia recalls: "One day Lía told us there was going to be an open retreat in a nearby parish and that if we wanted to we could go to do the prayer there and hear Mass. I would go and fetch Montse on those days and we went together. I remember the meditations the priest gave, opening up horizons of love for God and self-giving. Montse and I would look at each other and we prayed for the girls who attended."

In Llar they learned how to do the apostolate characteristic of members of Opus Dei: an apostolate of friendship and trust, service and self-denial;

of generous self-giving while not expecting anything in return; and of respect for the other's freedom, never seeking one's own interest or "using" friendship even for a noble end.

It was not particularly hard for her to carry out these principles. She knew how to be a friend to her friends; she knew how to give and to receive affection. She also realized that in doing apostolate she participated in the redemptive mission of Christ to save souls. It was a duty ("go therefore and preach the gospel") and a right. "Why am I going to get involved in other peoples' lives? Because Christ has gotten involved in your life and in mine!" the founder explained.

Her means of carrying out this mission were prayer, mortification, and a vibrant, resolute, apostolic activity. Her "allies" were her charm, good humor, and tennis.

Besides tennis there was basketball. She was on the school team, and they were playing a tournament. Now she had not just the incentive of the sport itself but also the apostolate. She had gotten to know a girl named Gloria, whom she wished to bring to the apostolate of the Work.

Gloria was a great sportswoman: she was the captain of a school team that was at the top of the tournament. She was a good student as well. One day Montse invited her to a meditation in Llar. After it finished, she asked her if she would like to think of going more frequently to the Center and having spiritual guidance from the priest, Fr. Julio González

Simancas. Gloria agreed. Montse was delighted and she said joyfully, "Do you realize what happened? Gloria has come. And she'll be back!"

Another one

Fr. Julio says: "I remember Montse as just another one of the girls who came to Llar." She did not do anything strange, anything that would be out of keeping with daily life in a Center of Opus Dei, where they put Christian living into practice. She went to daily Mass, she did half an hour of prayer in the mornings and another half an hour in the evenings; and sometimes she was seen to pray on her knees for the whole half hour.

She offered up her work before starting it; and, from the time of asking for admission to Opus Dei, she tried to do it with the maximum human and spiritual perfection. She read the New Testament regularly and other spiritual books. She said all three parts of the rosary. She paid a visit to the Blessed Sacrament. She tried to practice details of service to others. Everyone who knew her at this period of her life says the same thing: She was a person with great qualities but she did not look for attention. So, many days went by without her getting a mention in the Llar diary, which records the everyday events of the Center. There is only one brief reference on Tuesday, February 4: "After Mass, Montse spent the whole morning attending to oratory things."

This was her special job in the Center taking care of the oratory, preparing everything for the celebration of Mass. Obviously, at first they only gave her little jobs, for instance, to carry the ball when they were going to play basketball. She tried to be there first so the rest would not have to wait. Now she put all her love into the oratory task, because she realized it was related directly to God. Before beginning the job she would wash her hands as a small token of consideration for our Lord, before touching the liturgical objects, which would be in contact with the Body of Christ.

Her mother says, "Everything in her life was very small because the love of God is full of little things done for love... Everything very small, like the pain in her knee, which did not go away and was not particularly localized at first. Sometimes it hurt a bit higher up, then lower down." But she did not seem to care; she continued playing sports although it hurt. "Lame and all," she joked, "I will keep on playing."

It was a comment that made her human vigor very clear; she had learned it from her parents. Manolita recalls amusedly: "Kill or cure methods had become famous at home. When one of the children came home with some injury, Manuel would take the scissors, open the wound, disinfect it well, and that was that.... The child had to put up with the treatment as we had shown them how to be strong. That is why they were so surprised in Seva when one of their friends started to howl after he hurt himself and someone put a little disinfectant on the wound." Human courage was the foundation of supernatural fortitude, which would grow in her soul in the measure of her correspondence to grace. Fr. Julio says: "Fortitude can be of two types: the one the martyrs had, who died in one moment for the sake of love; and the other kind, which is dying to oneself little by little, through constant self-denial in little things. Montse's was of the second kind."

The early period of her vocation could be summarized in one word, happiness – total happiness in her recent, intensely acquired commitment. Lía recalls that in those early months, "her life developed peacefully. Like everyone else she had her trials with some failures and difficulties, but she always had tremendously sincere, transparent, interior beauty... She grasped everything with great ease and had a great love for her vocation."

She bubbled over with joy in her commitment, that profound joy God usually rewards generous people with at the outset of their vocation. Sylvia says: "In those early days in Opus Dei we often 'compared experiences,' and often we would find ourselves commenting on the Gospel passage of the rich, young man. We used to feel sorry for him. It seemed natural that he should go away sad because he had said *no* to our Lord because of his lack of generosity. On the other hand, how fabulous it was to have said *yes* to our Lord."

Paris in June

One day, early in February, when Montse was out, the Grases had visitors. They were Lía and the assistant director of Llar.

"They raised the possibility of Montse going to live at the Rouvray Residence, which was going to open in Paris. She could do a great apostolate among her companions there. They wanted to know what we thought of the idea," Manolita explains.

Although there were a few women of French nationality in Opus Dei, the Work had not yet established a stable apostolate with women in France. So it was to fall to Montse and a few others to begin the apostolic work in that country.

"We replied that if they thought it a good idea, we had no objections," Manolita continues. "Now we had to propose the idea to Montse.

"We liked the idea because we understood that, although there are sacrifices, following one's vocation to God gives immense satisfaction; and if one adds the fact of going to begin the activity in another country, the joy is even greater. We were sure that Montse would be delighted. She did not understand that there were some parents who placed obstacles in the way of God's plans. She said, 'How is it possible for there to be someone who does not want their daughter to have a vocation?'

"However, as there were still some months to go before putting these plans into action, we agreed, as Lía had suggested, not to propose any definite plan to Montse except the possibility of going to live in a Center of Opus Dei during the summer months.

"We began to get things ready. We talked about the clothes she might need, so that we could go and get them made and have everything thought out in time. I immediately bought some twill cloth and I started making lists of all the things she needed."

On February 12 Montse wrote to the founder again. It was near the anniversary of the beginning of the work with women of Opus Dei and Montse thanked God for it and for the apostolic fruit she saw in Llar. "Father, you cannot imagine how cheerful I am and how really happy I am."

A chocolate log

Meanwhile, as Montse was going deeper into her vocation, she was also increasing in gratitude to her parents. "The first seeds of faith, piety, and vocation are," the founder had explained "the result of their efforts in our hearts." "If I am like this," Montse said, "it is thanks to my parents."

She tried to show them her gratitude in different ways; and she tried to materialize it in some way, because now she saw clearly what the founder of Opus Dei had stated: that she owed ninety percent of her vocation to them.

She wanted to give them a present, but she did not have much money and the economic situation in

the family did not allow for any extravagance. The
only solution was to save up: that is to say
intersperse the trolleycar and subway trips with
walking. Coming and going from Llar in this way
she was able to get together five and a half pesetas.
It was not a big sum but sufficient to be able to buy
something from Cremel, the cake shop that displayed its tasty merchandise right next to the Llar
doorway – a chocolate log, which was her mother's
favorite cake.

That is all it was, a token of love for her parents. Just one more in the life of Montse. Maybe it
was not the most significant in her life, or the most
'heroic,' or the most transcendent, but it surely was
one of the most touching. And then she carried the
cake with such care – so it would not be squashed in
the rickety trolley. Wrapped in shop tissue paper, it
was also tied with a well-knotted cord, so she would
not drop it!

Easter 1958 – some snapshots in the garden

Her mother recalls: "We went, as always, to
Seva at the beginning of April to spend Holy Week
there. I was convinced that Montse would go to
France in the summer – although they had said
nothing to her yet; she foresaw going to live in a
Center of Opus Dei in the summer – so we wanted to
take advantage of her last holiday with us in Seva to
take some photographs in the garden of Villa Josefa

with the rosebushes in the background.

"We had to persuade her to let us take her photo. She was not keen on those photographic sessions; rather she was opposed to everything that meant standing out... She did not like to pose and would make faces to prevent us from taking her picture; in one of the photos she looks very comical making fun of the camera."

Montse's leaving home was going to be hard for her parents. "When I saw her so delighted with the idea of going to live in a Center of Opus Dei in the summer, I would say to her, now and again, pulling her leg:

'Montse you are dying to go... what nerve!'

'No, mom,' she would answer with a sweet, loving expression that made me understand the truth of her vocation."

In another letter to the founder, Montse referred to her mother's commentary. She said, "of course, she puts me on the spot; because, Father, you cannot imagine how happy we are at home. Mom and Dad are in the Work, and they are so good and I have spent such happy years with them."

Doubtful progress

"After the Easter holidays we returned to Barcelona," her mother continues. "Montse went on with her studies. But the pains did not stop, and I could see that her leaving was becoming more problematic. I even saw her uneasy at times….

"She carried on with her normal life: She attended class; she went to Llar; but even though she did not complain, you could see that it was increasingly difficult for her. She had dark circles under her eyes; it was clear she was not sleeping well, and she must have spent more than one night awake. The following morning I tried in vain to get her to stay in bed. But she got up punctually at the stipulated time even though she was exhausted. 'Montse, stay in bed, you have not slept at all.'

'No, mom.'

"And she got up."

The doctor thought that, with rest, the pain would go away. All she had to do was to get up a little later. But this was hard for Montse. She knew how much work there was in the house with so many brothers and sisters, and argued reasonably that when she got home from Mass her mother had done all the household chores and this was not right. They told her to offer up having to rest as a mortification.

Manolita observed that during lunch Montse would rub her knee surreptitiously with the tablecloth, and now and again her face would contort with a stab of pain. What could it be?

Seeing how things were, the family doctor recommended a visit to a specialist. On April 10 they went to the office of Dr. Escayola, who worked for the medical insurance company they were with. The doctor made a provisional diagnosis: "Rheumatic arthritis. Some slight hemorrhage." He ordered an X-ray.

But it did not seem to be a passing rheumatism. The knee continued to bother her, and on April 24 they returned to Dr. Escayola, who had the result of the x-ray which showed a slight separation of the periosteum.

Nowadays, any good medical student knows that a small separation of that type in the periosteum is a revealing sign – in medical language, pathognomonic – of a specific pathology, of a specific illness. But at that time it was not known what importance this might have.

On May 3 she returned to the doctor: the leg was a bit swollen and it hurt. Two days later the doctor decided to draw off some liquid. The result was negative. Clearly it was not arthritis but something else. The doctor put her leg in plaster. On the way out Montse was distraught.

The plaster went right down to her ankle, leaving her foot free; and even though Montse joked that she could wear ballet shoes, the fact is she got steadily worse. Besides, they had the impression that she had too thick a cast. But she put up with it.

She did not think it sufficient cause to change her schedule for the morning. Lía says: "Until she had to stay in bed, she did not miss going a single day to Llar to do the prayer. One felt such pity for her with her leg stretched out in the oratory; it was almost impossible for her to kneel, but she did some acrobatics to achieve it. 'Why not?' she said."

Next day her leg had swollen inside the plaster and the discomfort became intolerable. She said she could not stand it. Was she not exaggerating?

"Be a little more patient, Montse," someone said.

"Yes," she replied, smiling.

Everybody started to get uneasy. It did not seem to have been caused by a simple fall on a skiing trip... "On the third day, seeing the state she was in," her father says, "we decided to go to Dr. Esteva, a bone surgeon and a good friend. As soon as he saw her he said the cast should be removed at once and he would possibly put on a lighter one; but in any case be wanted to see her before she got a new one.

"They took the cast off. And this was very painful as the plaster had been put straight on to her skin... After the examination, Dr. Esteva told us the best thing was not to put anything at all on it. He revised the diagnosis and medication."

Her parents were puzzled. What could it be? What one doctor recommended the next one discouraged; and the following one did something else. They extracted fluid from the knee on several occasions but it was hard to say exactly where the pain was: the pain extended to the whole leg and, contrary to all prognoses, was getting worse. She complained of pain in her thigh, but they all said there was no reason to worry: the pain must be a reflex from some nerve or other.

May – a pilgrimage to Cisa

During the month of May some of the girls who went to Llar decided to do a pilgrimage to our Lady, saying all fifteen decades of the rosary, from Castelldaura to the shrine of Cisa, which is quite close. The way to get there was along a road of Mediterranean pines, with the ribbon of blue sea in the background all the time.

"I was to go by car," Rosa explains. "When we got there we would say another part of the rosary beside our Lady, and the third part on the way back." Lía said to Montse: "It is better for you not to walk as the doctor said you ought not use your leg much. You can go with Rosa."

Oh dear, she certainly did not like that one bit! She told Lía not to worry, that she would be able to walk that far...

"No, no, Montse," Lía said. "You go with Rosa in the car."

"Yes, come with me, you will keep me company," Rosa said.

"But I can walk like everyone else. I am not a cripple...!"

"But at that moment she realized that she might have hurt my feelings.... And then, without a moment's hesitation, she got into the car and said: 'Forgive me, Rosa. It was silly of me to say that because look, the most important thing is not being crippled on the outside, but being crippled on the inside: not being charitable and saying things that hurt others.'

I was really surprised and said, 'But you haven't really hurt me at all.' (It was true. I really had not noticed. I understood very well that she wanted to walk. I would love to have gone walking too...) How upset she was for having said that! And from that moment she made every effort to be kind to me.

"I know these are not major events. Everything I remember about her during this time is a little thing of this nature.... But, as the Father has taught us, these little things done for love of God are very important. When the Father learned that I wanted to be a pharmacist, he said: 'My daughter, when you are making up a prescription you can do it in two different ways: with love or with indifference. If you prepare it with affection and commend that person to God, she will leave with her prescription and your prayers.' Now, in the pharmacy every time I make up a prescription I remember it... What would my life have been if the Father had not taught me? Well this is what I admired in Montse: her love of God in these little things."

No chance of error

The weeks passed and her mother saw how her leg continued to hurt. "And one doctor said one thing then another and another, and the only thing we knew for sure was that they did not know the real cause of the pain. So we kept trying to find a good specialist." Until one day Adela, Manolita's sister, reminded her of Dr. Martin, a prestigious doctor friend who had seen Montse earlier on.

Dr. Martin examined her again. "Then," Manolita recalls, "it occurred to him to measure both thighs. He noticed a small difference in the movement of the muscle and said he wanted to have a radiologist friend of his do a series of x-rays.

"We went to the radiologist in question. I remember it perfectly. He took the pictures the doctor asked for in different positions. The time we spent in that room is engraved in my memory. I could see by the doctor's face that he was beginning to suspect something....

"Dr. Sáenz spoke to the specialist and he came to our home to talk to me. He spoke about a 'tumorous mass' and about doing analysis, etc.

'However, Doña Manolita, you mustn't think of something awful... although it may be serious.'

'So it's bad, Dr. Sáenz?'

'Yes, it is bad Madam. But we can put up a fight, you will see.'

"That was the end of my doubts. It was like clutching at straws attending to the vague half-truths the doctors had told me. And there were more visits to doctors.

"Dr. Martin called me on June 17 to say he had just studied all the X-rays and analyses that Dr. Roca had done. He told me not to worry. Comparing the movement of both legs, he too had feared the worst; but he had seen an improvement.... He insisted I should not worry, that in a few days time the whole diagnostic process would be complete. I am sure he said it good faith, he really believed that then. However, three days later....

"It was June 20, 1958, the first anniversary of the death of Carmen, the sister of the founder of Opus Dei.

"It was all very clear. There was no possibility of error; all our suspicious were confirmed. Montse had a cancer with no possible cure."

Manolita continues: "After the doctor had given his definite diagnosis and had taken away all hope of a cure, Manuel left the doctor's office saying:

'Look here, in spite of everything, I cannot lose hope. Above all the diagnoses we have the will of God.'

"When he came home he said nothing. I did not question him either. I looked into his eyes and read the whole story.

"Rafael was in bed with severe tonsillitis. I convinced everyone that I was worried about Rafael and that I feared it was not just tonsillitis but diphtheria... as I was sobbing uncontrollably.

"It was obvious now. It was a sarcoma, although as yet they did not know of what type: that, they would find out with a biopsy. There were conflicting opinions about this. Some doctors thought that one of the dangers of this disease was precipitating the process by stirring it up, even though the patient noticed an improvement, or I should say, a partial relief from the pain owing to decompression.

"On the other hand there was a tiny chance of a wrong diagnosis. What if it were all a mistake? Strange things do occur!"

❀   ❀   ❀

"I am getting lazy," Montse said to Lía, "so much so that whereas before I complained because I had to stay in bed, now there are days I feel so lazy about getting up. I don't think it is laziness, but drowsiness. I feel tired, but I don't know what from. Do you think that is normal? If you don't shake me up, I don't know what is going to become of me. You are all spoiling me!..."

Lía did not know how to handle that. She would have to wait for the result of the biopsy. Maybe it was all a big mistake. It was almost incredible to think... No, surely it was one big error. Let's just pray about it...

❀   ❀   ❀

Manuel Grases says: "In the end, after weighing the pros and cons, they decided to go ahead with the biopsy and we took her to the Red Cross Hospital where they looked after her very well. Dr. Jose Cañadell took care of her. He was a young doctor of about thirty five. He had acquired great prestige and was already the director of Orthopedic Surgery at the Red Cross Hospital."

June 26, 1958. At the Red Cross Hospital

Her mother recalls: "On June 26 we took her to the Red Cross Hospital. Montse was a bit frightened while waiting to go into the operating room. She was terrified of being there alone with the doctors. I explained to her my own experience on a particular occasion, when I had been operated on.

'Look, Montse. I, too, felt very lonely then, until I started to pray. Suddenly I felt sure that God was beside me, encouraging me, and giving me strength... you should pray too.'

"She went into the operating room. The doctor wanted to take a biopsy from the affected left femur. To do this he had to open the bone laterally four inches to facilitate the circulation of the blood and give some relief. I stayed outside walking up and down the corridor hoping and praying...

"Manuel had gone into the operating room."

Manuel takes up the story. "With Dr. Cañadell's permission I was wearing a white coat in the operating room, like a doctor. However, at one specific moment between one analysis and another, I could not control myself, and I gave Montse, lying asleep on the operating table, a kiss on her forehead. The nurses were taken aback; but I assured them immediately that I was her father..."

"There was a remote possibility that it was not so bad," Manolita continues, "and we prayed to God with all our might that it would be so...

"When they brought her back to her room, as she was recovering from the anesthetic, she kept saying: 'You were right, Mom. You were right!'

"I understood that God had accompanied her in those difficult moments.

"The doctors came. Dr. Roca had done all the analyses and the diagnosis was clear: Ewing's Sarcoma. They tried to comfort us. They said it was the most benign of all the sarcomas, how they would treat it, etc., etc....

"It was really hard, but we accepted God's will with all our hearts.

"We told Montse she had a tumor. Obviously we did not tell her the gravity of her situation. She accepted the news very well.

"It was the vigil of Sts. Peter and Paul. I remember how the two of us were in the hospital room, while outside we could hear a street party in full swing."

The following day some of the Llar girls went to Paris. Montse was supposed to have gone with them.

❀   ❀   ❀

"From my point of view," Rosa says, "Montse's heroicity lay in accepting with a smile, peace, and serenity... everything God sent her. This does not mean that she did not care. When she took a matter in hand, when she got excited about something, she would put her heart and soul into it....

"In this sense, as her illness progressed, I saw her evolve gradually. She stopped being impulsive: her youthful thoughtlessness abated and her bouts of bad temper became fewer and fewer."

They became fewer, not because they disappeared into thin air but because of her daily tenacious and determined struggle: a struggle that had its highs and lows, its successes and failures. But it was the positive striving of a person in love. "Today I will succeed with the grace of God," she would say, "tomorrow I will ask him again."

They spent three days at the Red Cross Hospital, from June 26 to 29. Manolita says: "When it was over we took her home. Getting her from the room to the taxi was very distressing. You could see her suffer. When we got home we installed her in a room at the far end of the corridor, which looks out onto Paris Street, near an image of Our Lady of Montserrat.

The girls who went to Llar got the news little by little. "For some days now we have been trying to cope with the news about Montse Grases," you can read in the Llar diary. "She has had cancer of the left leg diagnosed. They have not told her yet, but it seems they will have to tell her soon because it is progressing by leaps and bounds."

Ewing's Sarcoma

"Yes," Dr. Cañadell says, "the expression 'leaps and bounds' is not just expressive, but pretty accurate too. Montse was suffering from what we suspected at the beginning: Ewing's Sarcoma, a malignant tumor that occurs in young people between the ages of five and eighteen more or less, by far the most malignant of all the bone tumors. At that time from the signs of the first symptoms until death, the average life span was about a year and a half...."

In those days the only treatment that was of any use at all was radiation. It was possible to reduce the size of the tumor, but doctors were not really able to cure it.

There had been some talk of the possibility of using a drug, but it was still at a totally experimental stage. Surgery was out of the question. So the prognosis could not have been more gloomy....

Thirty sessions of radiation

Montse's father continues: "The radiation sessions began on July 2. The doctor prescribed thirty consecutive sessions every weekday, having a break on Saturdays and Sundays. We went to the radiology lab of Drs. Paris and Vilaseca, where she received the maximum dose of 10,000R."

"It was no easy task to get her there. It was difficult to get her into the taxi. I would put her leg along the back seat and sit in a corner. And the trip was only a block and a half.

"It seemed incredible to me that she preferred the complication of getting in and out of the car twice a day as well as the tedious wait in the street until we found a taxi, and I said as much several times. So much so that one day she agreed to walk since no taxi appeared. Poor child! The way she walked those few meters! I never said a word again! I can remember perfectly her grimace of pain when she arrived home."

She faced up to the discomfort of the taxi bravely. It was an ordeal to get her into the cars. In some of them she could stretch out her leg but not in others. But she did not make a fuss, she would say jokingly, "I need a made-to-order taxi."

Rosa and Ana María Suriol accompanied her a few times. Rosa recalls: "When we went for treatment, the nurses would ask what was the matter with her, but she would turn the conversation around and ask them about their lives. She became quite friendly with one of the nurses. She discovered she liked drawing and asked her about her sketches, or her problems with them... She would take advantage of the situation to do apostolate. She was on the ball!.... She was interested in everyone, even the doctor. She always asked one of us to stay with her during the session with the doctor. She found it a great comfort that we could be together.

"Sometimes when we were finished the nurse would say to me: 'How very friendly and cheerful your friend is. But I never know if she is in pain or not. Do you know?'

"I answered, 'No, I don't either.' "

Her parents did not know what to do. Was it more prudent to tell her how serious her illness was or to wait a bit? Did she suspect something? The doctors thought she could live for several more months. With all this time ahead, would it not be better to wait as their relatives suggested? Besides she was so looking forward to going to live in a Center of Opus Dei. How could they suddenly destroy these aspirations without hurting her unnecessarily? The doctors could be mistaken and instead of three months it might be ten, twelve, or maybe... who knows?

They decided to wait because although her leg was painful, Montse continued living a completely normal life. She knew she had a tumor but thought it would quickly shrink.... Lots of girls who knew her did not notice anything new in her. One says: "I saw her in Llar every Saturday, and I had no idea whatsoever that she was ill."

However, although they said nothing for the moment, the director of Llar and her parents agreed that they ought to prepare her. "Above all, spiritually," Lía specifies. "From then on I observed how she progressed in her interior life. She would ask me how she could practice virtue better in the little things. She grew in love for our Lady and she showed great sincerity in everything; and she would say everything with great simplicity."

Montse herself continued to be as happy as ever: playfully entertaining with a song in her heart. Rosa recalls, "She sang all kinds of songs. Pop songs, folk or traditional songs, like the one about the tall trees:

The heart that does not want to suffer pain
Spends its whole life free from love,
Free from love,
Ah my life, free from love."

A play

In Seva in those days everyone was talking about the play, *The House of Quirós*, by Carlos Arniches, which the children of the summer visitors were putting on that year in aid of the parish. They were under the wise tutelage of a Mr. Maqueda and made up a theatrical company entitled "The Grand Theatrical Company of Seva". They had had quite a successful performance the previous year with *Robbery in the Wilderness*.

We were all enthusiastic that Montse should take part and they gave her a script to learn her lines. You could see her on many afternoons in the garden, with her friend Marisa, going over and over the dialogue, trying to memorize the lines.

Her parents heard her say a particular passage, in a jocular tone, many times.

"This is not suitable for someone my age! Oh Mother of Mercy, I'm dying."

❀   ❀   ❀

"Do you know what is wrong with me?," Montse would ask Lía every time she went down to Barcelona. "I don't know anything, but I do notice how worried you all are?"

In accordance with Montse's parents wishes, Lía tried to prepare her.

"You never know what a tumor can be. Sometimes they are malignant. My father died because of one ..."

"But I am fine...."

"Maybe not, Montse... but we have to be prepared to do God's will. You know our bodies are a mystery. With all these tests they are trying to find out exactly what the matter is; but they can't find the cause of the pain... And no matter what the doctors do, God is the ultimate judge."

She had said as much as she could. Montse did not bat an eye. She simply said:

"I am in no pain at all now, Lía. Anyway I am ready to put up with whatever comes..."

Lía recalls: "Another day she asked me again, 'Why can't I know what the matter is? What do you think I have?'

"It was a real temptation for me to tell her what she had; yet, just thinking about it scared me... However little by little I did the ground work.

'Montse, are you really happy and prepared to accept whatever comes?'

"She answered: 'Of course I am. Why are you afraid? Look how strong I am.' And she showed me the muscles on her arms, 'I don't want you worrying about me.'

"But in spite of everything, you could see she was getting worse. Now and again she would seek me out and would ask me if I were very busy. I left off whatever I was doing at once, and we would sit down and chat a while. One day I resolved to speak more clearly to her, and during our conversation I said: 'You know some tumors develop into cancer.'

"I looked her straight in the eye to see what impact this caused. She continued to be calm and asked: 'If it is God who gave me my vocation, why shouldn't he give me health as well?'

"I could not contain myself and I said boldly: 'Are you sure you are ready for whatever should come?'

'Yes, yes of course. But I am very afraid of suffering and the doctors frighten me... but if God sends me more suffering as you say, he will help me a lot, just as you do.'"

Whatever You want

"This morning at Mass we remembered Montse in a special way," Lía wrote in the diary on July 10. "Today is her seventeenth birthday…. We thought that, maybe, precisely this was why our Lord wanted her for himself. She had given herself and there was no better gift than life itself, all her desires. She could, of course, have worked a lot... but we think that from heaven she will help us much more."

They celebrated Montse's birthday in Llar with fun and games and songs. Lía wrote in the diary: "Rosamaría Pantaleoni and Carmen Salgado came early to make a 'mural' for her, with a lot of love. We prepared a surprise for her for the afternoon. After her visit to the doctor she will come here and we will have a great get-together."

Seventeen! Time passed and her parents agreed with Lía that she should be getting ready for death.... The time had come to speak clearly about her situation. She had just a few months of life left, yet she kept talking about how this year she would be doing this and next year that...!

The time was ripe. Now.

It was easy to say "the time is ripe." How should we do it? How should we break the news – which is hard even with older people – to a girl who feels her young life bubbling in her veins.

Lía tried again. Right now with the radiation treatment in full swing, Montse felt much better. The sessions were lengthy at first, then moderated progressively, until they lasted just a few minutes. This was the moment to act. On July 18, a Friday, before going to Seva with her parents, they were talking in Llar. Lía thought: "Maybe it will be easier than we imagine. Maybe she realizes everything and doesn't dare tell us...."

They chatted about several things. Lía did not know how to begin. At last she told Montse how the founder's sister, Aunt Carmen as she was known affectionately by the members of the Work, had died.

"Montse, you know Aunt Carmen suffered a lot before she died. She had an illness like yours..."

"What did Aunt Carmen die from?"

"Cancer."

Lía looked Montse in the eye. At that instant, in a single second, she realized that Montse had not realized anything at all.

"Yes, but I don't have cancer..."

❈   ❈   ❈

She went back to Seva with her parents. There she asked her parents what illness she had. What had Lía meant to say to her. However it was not possible to talk peacefully in Seva, surrounded by children and friends. They had to take care of the little one, the twins, and the older ones who would get up to all kinds of mischief....

Her mother recalls: "We agreed to tell her when we got back from Seva, when we would be just the three of us so we could talk peacefully."

They returned to Barcelona on Sunday evening. Normally they got a lift with Mr. Maqueda, or sometimes with Mr. Brosa who was holidaying nearby in Taradell, both friends of Manuel.

Her mother relates: "That weekend Brosa sent us a message saying that he was not going; so we had to take the train, which was very full. Manuel managed to get a seat for Montse in the corridor, of the kind used by the ticket inspector. But the train was so crowded that she had great difficulty finding a position for her leg. What awful things happen sometimes! We were not going to explain the situation to everyone.... She would have suffered even more... and we made the trip in this distressing fashion."

They got into Barcelona very late because the train was held up. The city was engulfed in the hot silence of summer.

They opened the door into the house. The sitting room clock struck. It was 12:30 a.m... They started getting ready for bed.

Her mother continues: "Montse then came to me and said:

'Well, Mom, are you going to tell me what I've got?'

'But, Montse, at this time of night...?'

'Yes. We're not putting this off any longer. Tell me right now what I've got.'

"I realized we could not delay it any further. Manuel explained everything to her briefly but clearly, not mincing words.

'Montse, you have cancer. Ewing's Sarcoma.'

"She was startled for a second and inquired:

'Couldn't they cut my leg off?'

"Manuel told her there had been a consultation on that aspect; they had considered everything, but that possibility was out, it could not be....

"Then she made a gesture, a frown, as if saying, 'what a pity!'

"It was just a gesture; to me it seemed a gracious gesture after hearing such dreadful news, poor darling... and she went out of the room to her own room.

"I saw how she knelt down at the feet of Our Lady of Montserrat and began to pray.

Then she sat down to do a brief examination of conscience. She said three Hail Mary's on her knees and got into bed. Then I said to Manuel: 'I am going to her.' I thought she would not be able to sleep after hearing such a thing....

"I went to her room and I pushed her over a bit to make room for me in her bed, and she said:

'Mom, what are you doing?'

'Well, look here, sleeping with you.'

'Gosh, I am lucky!' she said jovially.

She rested her head on my shoulder and after a few minutes, literally, she was breathing deeply. I realized she had gone to sleep.

"I checked to be sure she was asleep and left her. And that is all.

"... Not quite all, because later on I found out that on kneeling down in front of Our Lady of Montserrat she had said: "Whatever You want."

❀   ❀   ❀

"...I know these are but a few words to describe such a big thing as explaining her illness to Montse. However, there is nothing to add. It was as simple as I have said. She did not even know about the existence of such an illness, since not so much was known then as now. I do not believe she had the slightest inkling of her disease. I remember perfectly well her facial expression... just that frown, no tears in her eyes... nothing at all. How supernatural it was!

"Supernatural. I have been hesitant about using that word. But it fits. If not, what word can I use? What a "strange" thing? What an "abnormal" thing? No. She always acted normally and naturally. Evidently God comforted her... Because if he took all her dreams and everything away so suddenly... would he then leave her on her own?

"I always saw the hand of God in all the events of those days and I felt him very close to me several times. From that moment on Montse realized that she could not fulfill any of her desires, full of enthusiasm as she was, thinking there were just a few days left before going off to live in a Center of Opus Dei; and this was the only thing that sometimes made her impatient. Earlier she realized her illness was dragging on and she said so anxiously.... That night her misgivings were confirmed. She would never fulfill the dreams that had carried her along these last months.

"Next day, Monday, first thing in the morning, I called Lía to tell her everything, unbeknown to Montse. Later on, Montse and I went to Monterols for confession. Fr. Gonzalo Lobato, the priest, warned me not to give Montse an impression of being an invalid; even though it was hard, I was to treat her normally.

"Normally! And the fact is I believe I did.... How? With God's grace."

"I was in Monterols that morning," Carmiña Cameselle recalls, "and I saw Montse after her conversation with the priest. I realized she had been crying. But she said nothing, only, 'I am going to Llar.' And she left."

When she was happiest

"I remember perfectly well that morning when she came to Llar," Roser recounts. "I opened the door for her. She asked me if Lía was at home. I told her she was in her office talking with someone. She greeted our Lord in the oratory and knocked on Lía's door saying:

'Lía I want to talk to you, when you are ready. Meantime what would you like me to do?'"

Lía was moved, but she controlled herself; she told Montse to do some ironing of oratory linen.

The time had come, Lía thought. First of all Lía went to the tabernacle to ask our Lord for the strength to be able to have this conversation. Meanwhile she could hear something that surprised her a lot. It was the cheerful voice of Montse singing in the ironing room.

When I was happiest
Without thinking of your love,
You wished me to love you;
And I did so, passionately.

And I will go on loving you
Even after I die
Because I love you with my soul
And my soul is immortal

Because I love you with my soul
And my soul is immortal.

Lía says: "I heard her singing peacefully; so much so that I feared they had told her so delicately that she had not taken it in. We started talking. I was trying to appear calm, although I am not sure if I achieved it because Montse asked me:

'Have you been crying Lía? Well, you know that I know everything, even the fact that I am going to die soon. Dad told me yesterday….'

'What do you feel Montse?'

'I accept it. I have just been to confession and I am very peaceful.'

"She told me what the priest said to her: 'He said I was very lucky because I was going to enjoy God soon. Just imagine, at first I did not think so, but now I do. I am very peaceful and happy. I really am at peace. I want God's will. Remind me in case I forget, I want God's will. This is the second time I give myself to God. I have already done it once.

'Mom says I should ask Isidoro to cure me. What do you think? I get very mixed up at times. Sometimes I want him to cure me; other times I think not, that if it is what our Lord wants, it is his will. When I get into this mess I say to our Lady she should fix it as she wants. Don't you think that's the best thing?'

"Then she told me about the conversation she had had with her parents. She said she realized how they had suffered when they told her about her illness and how they must be very holy if our Lord was asking them for this sacrifice.

'Mom thought I would say something to her but nothing occurred to me. I felt an internal shiver and I just thought I had to be strong.'

"She also said we were foolish for not having told her before.

'Rascal! Imp! So you knew all along and you didn't tell me...! I know you have suffered a lot. Now I can understand all the worry and fuss, here as well as at home. I could not understand it. Now I know what I've got, I'm at peace.'

"We spoke about death in the most serene way. She found it hard to come to terms with the idea: 'Well, because I have no pain at all, do you know? '

"We talked about pain, too, which she accepted 'as a purification to get to heaven.'

'I accept it,' she went on. 'I am very selfish. Do you know that up to now I have been praying for my health. I shouldn't pray for that. Should I?'

'And what are you praying for now?'

'I am praying for the fulfillment of God's will. That way I will be much more peaceful.'

"Then she took Aunt Carmen's picture and while she held it in her hands we talked about her last illness. When I told her how much she had suffered and how holy she had been, she pleaded with me for all of us to help her. 'I want to be as brave as she was.'

"I asked her then what thought passed through her mind when her father gave her the news. She answered that she had taken the crucifix into her hands and kissed it saying, '*Serviam*, I will serve you Lord, I will be faithful to you...'

"Then she added: 'Tomorrow I am going to write to the Father telling him everything, so he can pray for me; and I am going to tell him: I am going to offer everything up for Opus Dei.'

"Then her eyes filled with tears as she got to the heart of the matter and said:

'So now I can't be a numerary, can I?'

"Her face lit up when I said: 'But Montse, whoever told you that? We want you to be a numerary and a very holy one at that. That is why you did the Admission the other day.'

"She answered: 'I will be. I promise.'

"I saw her so peaceful, as if she had matured all of a sudden, that I even told her of the plan we had had for her to go to Paris.

'But look Montse,' I said, 'from today on let us commend this project to God even though you yourself won't be going.' "

     ❀   ❀   ❀

Lía wrote that night in the diary: "Blessed Communion of Saints, which makes a woman out of a girl, a person conscious of the difficult ordeal that our Lord had sent her and that she has accepted cheerfully!"

6

A big leap forward

"It was then that she made a big leap forward," her brother Enrique recalls. "Up to then her
life had been mostly the consequence of the
Christian education we had received at home. But
then she came face to face with this dreadful phe-
nomenon of pain. It was then that she became identified with Christ on the cross. She discovered she
was condemned to die, in a manner of speaking, in a
short while; so she began to be heroic in the little
things and to put into practice the teaching of the
love of God in the midst of suffering that we all
know about, but that we can only truly live when we
experience sorrow in our own flesh."

Montse wrote to the founder on September 2:
"I am aware of the help you send me because I find
myself happier and more peaceful with each passing

day. I don't want to avoid anything, but I wish to offer our Lord everything for the Work.

"Father, I wish you to know that I was supposed to have gone to Paris.... I am reminded of this by the fact that you have been there recently, and you can imagine how I am praying for the apostolate there to be very successful."

❁   ❁   ❁

She returned to Seva where she continued to take part in family activities as far as her new circumstances permitted. She took full advantage of feeling much better after the radiation treatment to visit her friends who were spending the summer nearby.

She continued to live her plan of life regularly: Holy Mass, prayer... in many, various circumstances. María Luisa Xiol can remember her saying the Angelus everyday at noon. When they were swimming, they would get out of the water to say this prayer in honor of our Lady. Then they would return to their enjoyment, splashing about. Carmen Salgado recalls too how she went to confession punctually, every single week, and the devoted way she got ready for it was noticeable. "It seemed to me she went very deep, if her external attitude was anything to go by." She carried on with the same vitality as ever: she even learned to play a piece or two on Rosa Pantaleoni's accordion.

The news of "Montse's condition" spread among the families in Seva gradually. They would talk discreetly in groups, and whisper it over the evening get-togethers. From there it spread to the church door, the bread shop, the grocer's... Balbina Garrido was at the grocer's. She had helped Manolita with the housework for the past few years and there she was, waiting her turn. The Grases had not told Balbina yet about the severity of Montse's illness so as not to upset her. A lady approached.

"What a ghastly thing, Montse's cancer, isn't it?'

"What on earth do you mean? Cancer. Who said Montse had cancer.'

"Oh, forgive me! But it is what everyone in the village is talking about.'

Balbina returned to Villa Josefa absolutely furious. "These villagers are all the same! Someone has a bad leg and everyone begins to gossip about cancer. They don't know what to say next!" And off she went to tell Manolita:

"Do you realize what they are talking about in the village, Mrs. Grases? Nothing less than Montse's trouble being cancer!'

Montse was listening and laughing.

"Look here, Balbina," Manolita began to explain.

A trip to Lourdes

Rosa relates: "About that time I decided to go to Lourdes. So I said to Montse, 'Do you know what? I have never particularly wanted to go to Lourdes because deep, deep down I haven't really believed that I might be cured there. If I were to go I would be lacking in faith. You know well that I have faith in our Lady, but to think of suddenly being cured... I find that very hard to believe, I am sorry to say.

'But now I am going to go because now there is something much more important. When I am there and I take the baths I am going to ask our Lady for your cure.'

"Then we established our priorities: My polio was subordinate to her cancer. And she recognized that on this occasion it was more important to pray first of all for her and later on for me. But we decided this like someone who has solved a logistical problem, as if we had said, 'OK, this evening I will see you at seven at Lezo's.' And off I went to Lourdes to fulfill my part of the bargain... to pray with all my heart, to take baths with all the faith I could muster, as well as the desire, the joy, and the hope that our Lady would cure Montse.

"However, when I got to Lourdes and got into the baths something very strange happened to me. I did not remember her leg or my own. I only asked our Lady to give Montse the best, that she should be happy. Then I wrote to her telling her about the sick, about their resignation, the impressive silence at the Grotto despite the fact we were thousands, the love for our Lady, the poignant blessing of the sick in the esplanade, the concern of the 'brancadiers,' the torchlit procession, the fervor..."

Rosa believes that Montse was praying for a cure for herself from Barcelona at the same time. But when she realized it was not God's will she accepted it joyfully, making no fuss at all. She never did like making a fuss. When people asked her about her illness she evaded the issue.

"She used to try to think of others," Rosa explains, "and did not like to talk of her aches and pains... as she did not consider them to be so bad. One day she said to me:

'Rosa, you used to talk to me so much about the cross and now I have it... Now when I look at it, I look at it lovingly, really you were so right, it is our cross, yours and mine....'"

Back to school again

Summer was over and it was time for the next academic year at *L'Escola*. Montse was perfectly aware of the seriousness of the situation but did not hesitate for a second in signing up for another year... although she was quite sure it would be the last one. One of the teachers was an aunt of Carmen Salgado and she made an effort to see Montse and ask her how she was. Montse evaded the question. "Fine,

fine," she answered.

Most people in her situation would despair or at least be mournful or apathetic or abandon their aspirations... all of which is normal. Not so in Montse's case. She tried to fulfill her calling faithfully right up to the last minute. She knew her vocation urged her to sanctify each day's work; so she enrolled in September for a course she knew she would not finish...

Her friends were amazed. "She began to make plans, as to what she was going to do, as if nothing was the matter," Carmen Salgado recalls. "She said: 'I will study piano; let's see if I have time to finish the course, that would please my parents. But I must ask Ana María for the books, as it would be a pity to have them spend all that money for a few days.'"

She was never "a special case"

She did her best to live normally... as far as her strength permitted. "One day I was going along on a Vespa with a sidecar," Roser recalls, "and I saw her, as I often did, at the bus stop on Balmes Street going towards Tibidabo Hill. Her leg was quite swollen at this stage. As soon as I saw her I said:

'Do you want a ride?'

'I do', she said smiling, 'but I don't know if my leg does.'

"Then she hitched her leg into the sidecar with a big effort and sat down as best she could. I was surprised at the joy with which she did these things even though it was hard on her. But I did not think much about it: she always seemed a very normal girl to me....

"However, I realize now, with hindsight, that the extraordinary part of Montse's behavior lay precisely in her normality. She had the ability to endure her illness without attracting attention to herself; she did not try to be the center of attention and gave no importance at all to her illness.... When we asked her about her illness she would respond without either exaggeration or frivolity in the same tone as one might say... 'I had an exam this morning and I did quite badly.' Seeing her like this, joyful and happy although she was going to die shortly, helped us to see it as normal.... She never wanted to be 'a special case' though she could have perfectly well been considered so, considering that she was so young and, of all the girls who went to Llar, the only one who was ill."

Ana María Suriol says, "She did not want to talk about death as it seemed like talking about herself."

"Of course, it was not only due to her own merits but to the grace of God that she responded to so well," Roser continues. "However, we must not forget that she did not discover the seriousness of her illness just at that time. She knew about it for many months. I remember asking her at one point how she was and she said quite frankly.

'Well, they say I won't make it to Christmas.'"

Orange or turquoise?

Her mother was baffled by Montse's attitude. One day that summer, the dressmaker came to make a dress for Montse and she could not decide which material to choose. There were two patterned materials, one turquoise and the other orange. Her mother looked on in amazement. Her daughter's indecision confirmed her suspicions. Montse must think she was going to get better; otherwise her hesitations, her fussing about it, made no sense....

"'Why is she taking so long in choosing her dress?' is what I was thinking," her mother recalls. "What on earth does it matter what it is? How can this daughter of mine be having these doubts at this stage, as if she were going to be wearing the dress this summer and the next and the one after that?"

"Montse went on looking at the materials and examining them. 'The fact is that this one is lovely but this other one...'

"And I continued saying to myself," Manolita says, "'It cannot be! Can she have forgotten what we said to her? I don't think so...'

"Then I bumped into her in the corridor and asked:

'Listen here Montse, Dad is sure you are going to get better. Sometimes I think so too. What about you?'

"She did not answer.

'Tell me what you think,' I insisted, 'you never say anything.'

"She looked at me with a big peaceful smile on her face.

'I never think about it,' she said, as if to indicate she had abandoned herself completely into God's hands."

She surprised everyone who knew her in the same way. And those who did not know what she had, would never have guessed the seriousness of her situation. Jean Marie was a French boy who did an exchange with Enrique. He came again to spend some time in Seva as he had done the previous year and quickly became involved in the family life.

Manuel Grases recalls: "Now and again he would tease Montse about her swollen leg, not even remotely suspecting what she had. She would just smile at him and say nothing."

"The same thing happened on the big feast day in Seva," María Luisa recalls. "We went up the bell tower of the church to hear and see the sardanas from up there. We were quite some time just contemplating the scene. I could see that it was a farewell for her, to see and feel all these things for the last time.... But she said nothing and down we came."

Clearly Montse hated being dramatic.

The House of Quirós

She hated being dramatic but she loved dramatic art. That summer she took part in the play that the "Grand Theatrical Company of Seva" put on. The children of the summer visitors set up this company with the pompous name as a joke.

The performance took place on September 24, the feast of Our Lady of Ransom. The play, *The House of Quirós*, by Carlos Arniches, tells the story of the adventures and misfortunes of two young people in love who have to defend their love against the social mores of the day. There was a certain amount of social criticism in the play which had lost impact over the years, but fortunately the best part of his work remained intact. Montse played the part of the aged housekeeper of a traditional, old Castillian manor house.

The first scene starts off with verve. Montse, that is Doña Cástula, is chatting to Librada, a cheeky servant, and to Modesta. She gets entangled two minutes later with Sol – played by María Luisa Xiol – who has lost her appetite. She had to control her laughter and pretend to be very bad tempered when the peasant Lucio appeared. He was talking in his own particular slang, which was not exactly academic, about what had happened to him in the big city:

Lucio: We went into the dining room for lunch and after lunch everyone started to put little wooden sticks in their mouths and suck them. I said to myself, "they must be sweet," so I took one and for half an hour I sucked and sucked until I had to throw it away. I didn't taste anything at all, even though I chewed it well.

Sol: For goodness sake, those were toothpicks.

Lucio: Whatever you say, but they ought to cook them.

Sol: What blissful ignorance!... Imagine eating toothpicks!

Doña Cástula: I have never seen such ignorance!

The plot thickens. Casimiro and Sol look for a stratagem so the terrible Don Gil will grant his daughter's hand. But he does not budge. *"The hand of a Quirós del Pulgar Carillo de Penas Altas will be granted only to a nobleman,"* he yells!

However Casimiro is not to be intimidated: "You can give her hand to whoever you wish," he protests, "but the lady in question has offered the rest to me."

The scene becomes more complicated by the minute amid much laughter from the public, right up to the second act (which we will not reveal so as not to deprive the reader of the pleasure of reading it). Montse opens the scene shouting:

"Oh dear! This is not suitable for someone of my age! Oh mother of Mercy I am dying!"

Montse knew now perfectly well what she was saying. A sad shudder ran through the whole audience.

❀   ❀   ❀

"I did not expect Montse to act so well or so naturally," her mother said on the way out of the parish theater. There were congratulations and good wishes for the whole company. It was a delightful evening; but Montse arrived back at Villa Josefa exhausted.

"It was the feast day of Our Lady of Ransom when she started to have the pain again," her mother recalls. "And I say this with all due respect: it never occurred to me to think it could have been any other day."

It was precisely that day, while everyone was laughing at Doña Cástula's witticisms, that suffering entered her life again. And it never left her. Montse had achieved something more than just concealing her pain; she had converted it into joy and laughter. No one could suspect her suffering while everyone enjoyed her acting.

October 2, 1958

"I only saw her sorrowful once," her mother continues. "It was October 2, the thirtieth anniversary of the foundation of Opus Dei. Montse went to Llar to celebrate the feast and precisely that day the pain got worse. It was after the meditation, during the get-together, when she began to feel bad. She realized that she might spoil the feast day for them; so she decided to leave discreetly, not telling anyone she was going...."

"I was afraid I would not be able to get home," she told Lía the next day, "and I wanted to take a taxi, but trying to live poverty, I didn't."

"When she came home," her mother recalls, "she came in with a big smile and she seemed very bubbly. She knew we were going to the cinema and she did her best not to let us know."

'I suppose,' she said, 'you are having dinner early so you can go to the cinema with Dad.'

"However, when she went to set the table, which she used to do every day, she was not able to cope and she had to sit down on a chair. She asked her sister Pilar to do it for her; and Pilar came running to tell me. I found her lying down in her room...

"We had a chat that I find myself quite incapable of putting into words. She insisted that we should go to the cinema, that nothing was wrong, that she was fine... until tears came into her eyes with the pain. We did not go out of course, but we did celebrate the feast very much in God's presence."

A homily in the parish

Pius XII died in the early hours of October 9. "The Pope is a saint," Montse said when she heard the news.

Some weeks later, on October 28, the white smoke that came out of the chimney of the Sistine Chapel announced to the world at large the news everyone had been waiting for, that a new pope had been elected with the name of John XXIII.

It was a time of joy and prayer in the whole Church for the new pontiff. The newspapers were giving us the first biography of the new pope, speaking of his great humanity and his pleasant smiling face. He was the favorite topic of conversation in family get-togethers and in parish sermons. But in that month of November some priests at least preferred to speak of the theme of the month, related to the feast of All Saints and All Souls.

Manolita recalls: "I shall never forget November 9 that year…. That day, Sunday, for different reasons we did not go to Mass at our parish church as was our custom, but to 10:00 Mass at the parish of Nuria. The priest began his sermon talking about death: the rigor mortis of the dead body, the coffin, the grave, etc. He gave us an example so we could get used to the idea and not be apprehensive. 'Let us imagine,' he said, 'that one of you is ill with a tumor in the leg. It is a cancerous tumor, which causes a lot of suffering and naturally will destroy the life of that person. The doctor orders the leg to be amputated. This means the person is freed from a member that caused him much suffering. Don't you think he will watch the burial of that part of his body, which caused him so much suffering, with a smile on his face? That is how the soul will watch the burial of the body, also the cause of pain and sin, from heaven!'

"Tears were rolling down my face... But Montse, who was sitting in front of us with some of her brothers and sisters, turned around to me with a big smile of amusement and made a gesture as if saying, 'If he only knew...'

"It was one of the few times she saw me crying.... The truth is that her illness provoked a lot of tears... but so as not to sadden her or anyone else, I tried to be cheerful and never to cry in front of her. I think I achieved this with the help of our Lady."

A conspiracy of silence

In this kind of situation it is hard to know what to do. It is difficult to be natural with a person who is going to die soon. One often has recourse to a "conspiracy of silence" on the theme in question. People whisper in corners, they make guarded gestures, they avoid references.... Balbina, the woman who helped Manolita with the household chores, as soon as she found out what was going on, made everyone carry out this conspiracy of silence to the bitter end. Montse, though, did not care two hoots; actually, she was amused. Her mother says: "I remember one occasion she was rinsing out her stockings, and mine as well, and she said, 'Mom, Balbina was very upset a little while ago. Ignacio came in telling how his friend's father had just had his third operation for cancer. Balbina said: 'Hush, we don't talk about that here! Hush!' 'What nonsense!' Ignacio said. 'Hold your tongue,' she threw back at him. 'I think Balbina cares more about me now; she must think I am not going to last long. Look these are your stockings and these are mine. Don't mix them up.' She said all this at one go, while she has hanging the stockings on the shower rail."

Her indifference was not because of a lack of awareness. Montse was not frivolous; she knew perfectly well that her days were numbered. She had said as much herself. But she was living with the same serenity as if she had years to live. She studied, prayed, helped in the house, went out with her friends. Or perhaps it was, precisely because she knew she did not have much time, she wanted to live it faithful to her vocation as God wanted her to live. She carried on normally; "anyone in my place, of my age, and belonging to Opus Dei would do the same," she said to her mother.

"She carried on normally, that is true. But not to complain when you could see by her face perfectly well the pain she was suffering...!" This is what Encarna Ramos could not understand. Encarna had been helping her mother with household chores for some years. She had known Montse from the age of seven. She could see her suffering a lot. Encarna says: "When I was pondering on her suffering, Montse often said to me: 'I have not suffered enough yet to go to God and to be with him. I have to suffer more.'"

❀   ❀   ❀

Apparently nothing had changed.... On a lot of Sunday afternoons she still went to the Suriols' house. Jorge Suriol says: "She participated fully, pulling people's legs, and I enjoyed this a lot. Her cheerfulness astonished me. Her discretion did too...; not that she hid her illness, but she never showed what was happening to her. I knew, through my family, what she had in her leg and really I was very impressed that she did not talk about it.

"Her example helped me a lot, as far as I allowed it to: because at that time, due to the misleading information I had about the Work, I maintained a strong critical spirit against it. And I did not just 'think'; I also said it both to my sister and to Montse. I criticized their way of acting and I made all kinds of unpleasant jokes about Opus Dei and their apostolate...

"It was some years before I understood Opus Dei, which was thanks to a meeting with the founder in 1963, when God also granted me a vocation. But at the end of the fifties I had a very negative image of the Work – with just one exception, Montse. She was the only one who sweetened the image...."

Rosa concludes: "It is quite true; she was never sad. She was as nice as always and never lost her sense of humor. She saw the bright side of everything and she always had a funny story at hand to tell. She always made me laugh."

7

An unexpected surprise

"Encarnita Ortega, Central Secretary of the women's section of Opus Dei, came to Barcelona in the early part of November that year. There was a get-together in Llar and she told them the latest news of the apostolic activity from Rome and all over the world," Manolita recalls.

"I was able to meet Encarnita too, and I suggested to her how wonderful it would be if Montse could meet the Father.. but if it were not soon, she would not be able to go at all. Encarnita promised me she would look into it as soon as she got back to Rome. And she did, as they sent us word almost immediately that Montse should come. How delighted Montse was when we told her!"

Rome! Near the Pope! Meet the Father, the founder of Opus Dei! Just like that, in a few hours time! She had never even dared to dream about it. And now there it was, within arm's length! She could not believe it. Who would have said such a thing a few weeks earlier, that she, Montse, would be in Rome!

"Montse made the journey on her own for two reasons," her mother explains. "One of them, the main one, was that we thought that by going alone she would have a better chance of living family life in one of the Centers of Opus Dei; whereas if I went, she would have to stay with me. As I was sure she would wish to live immersed in that atmosphere, even for a few days, we thought it best to do it that way. The other reason– although it took second place – was financial."

"How happy she was, going to Rome!" Rosa recalls. "She was limping. Her parents and Lía accompanied her to the airport. Off she went with her suitcase. When she was just going to board the aircraft she turned around and waved, smiling, beaming with anticipation!"

A violent storm

Her mother says: "Something happened on the journey that I did not count on at all. It was a mystery. I think it was another trial that our Lord permitted to happen to her. The upshot is that in spite of Manuel's efforts to have one of the flight attendants take care of her, not only did they not attend to her, but they made her get out of the aircraft at both stopovers, in Nice and Milan....

"Worse still, at one of the landings, after making her get out and walk from the aircraft to the airport buildings in her desperate situation, they asked for her passport. She had to return limping to the aircraft to get it, in pouring rain, and back again.

"The flight was very bad, especially the one between Milan and Rome. The aircraft was almost empty and they flew into a thunderstorm. One of the passengers became hysterical and started screaming. From what she told me later the air hostesses did not worry about the passengers at all. They stayed in their cabin and did not bother to come out.

'And what did you do?' I asked her.

'I thought that here I was, over Rome, and maybe I would not get to see the Father after all....'"

This thought was not provoked by pessimism. Montse oozed optimism and *joie de vivre*. But, during her lifetime, she had seen how all her human desires, one after another, had come tumbling down. "Do you realize," she asked her mother, "how everything I have set my heart on in this life, I have had to leave behind. When I was happiest in the Jesus and Mary School; you moved me; then, again, I had to leave the Dominicans. Later I had to stop playing basketball because of the tumor, and now, since I am a member of Opus Dei..."

Now that she was a member of Opus Dei all she had left were just a few months of life and the desire to meet the founder himself. She had given her life to God in Opus Dei, in the service of the Church; would God ask her to give up that too? She was ready....

No, God did not ask for that. Those days in Rome were, without doubt, the happiest days of her life, in spite of the physical pain.

The founder had given precise and specific instructions to ensure that they should be happy days. Martha Sepúlveda, a Mexican girl who lived in Villa Sacchetti, recalls that he told her to show Montse the whole Center in great detail, including all the oratories; to see to it that she sat at a table with people of many different nationalities so that she could hear stories of the apostolic activity of Opus Dei in their respective countries; to sing Mexican songs in the get-together because he knew she was very fond of them; and even though, at that time, he did not usually have his photograph taken with visitors, he made an exception for Montse. Martha recalls: "He wanted us to do our best to make sure that she enjoyed those days, 'anticipating her every wish.' He told us that 'we should guess her thoughts.'"

Pepa Castelló recalls: "Icíar Zumalde, Milena Brecciaroli, and I went to Ciampino Airport to fetch her in the middle of a thunderstorm. I remember that as soon as the plane landed there was a flash of lightning and the whole airport was plunged into darkness for a few minutes...."

Montse felt a bit faint so they sat down until she recovered. Encarnita Ortega recalls: "Then some

reporters came up and asked if she were a film star."
Obviously they had been attracted by the cheerful
reception she had received and her good looks....

Pepa carries on: "As soon as she arrived,
while Icíar was picking up the suitcase, Montse told
me how she had been terrified during the journey
because of the storm, and how she had made many
acts of contrition because she thought she was going
to die at any minute. Then she began to show me the
photographs of her family, which she had brought to
show the Father....

"We went straight to Villa della Palme. She
lived there during the few days she spent in Rome.
Some members of the household were waiting to
welcome us. They had prepared a special room for
her. It was a small sitting room, which had been
converted into a bedroom, so that she would not
have to climb any stairs. The room was very near the
oratory, and it had a bathroom next door. I helped
her unpack and she showed me everything she had
brought: the photograph, the dresses and jerseys her
mother had tailored to look like new."

They advised her to rest a little that Wednesday so as to recuperate after such a long, tedious
journey. Encarnita Ortega went to Villa delle Palme
first thing in the afternoon to spend some time with
her. After having a chat they went to the Vatican.
Although they saw she was tired, they did not prevent her from visiting the Basilica of St. Peter on her
first day in Rome, so as to fulfill the wish of every
pilgrim who comes to the very heart of Christianity.

Encarnita recalls: "Montse displayed her usual enthusiasm and was impressed by the size of the Basilica, its artistic beauty, and its great significance for Catholics. We said the Creed; we did the usual tour. I remember we stopped in front of the statue of St. Peter and asked him for the knack he had – being able to convert three thousand souls at his first sermon. It was a short, intense visit and we prayed particularly for the Church and the Pope. On her return to Villa delle Palme, Montse was radiant."

Meeting the Father

Pepa continues the story. "The next day, Thursday, at 10:30 a.m., we arrived at Villa Sacchetti where the Father received her."

For the occasion Montse decked herself out in her finest outfit. Encarnita says: "She was wearing high-heeled shoes, although it was a big effort because of her illness, and she was wearing a new pale-blue jersey, which suited her perfectly.

Encarnita goes on: "The Father asked her about her trip and about her family. He also asked her what she had seen of Rome and what we had shown her of the central house. He told her to ask God for health, as health is a good, and that she should promise our Lord that if he granted it, she would always be faithful. But she should also add that she accepted his will totally."

Manolita tells: "The Father told her he wanted

her to get better and how he would pray for her to get well, although he accepted God's will in everything. He said the same thing again later on that morning on the phone to Encarnita. He insisted also that Montse should know that he desired her cure with all his soul.... He gave her a present of rosary beads, a prayer card, and a medal. He wanted a photograph taken with her and Don Alvaro in the place called Galleria del Torreone. Icíar is on the right of the photo and Encarnita is on the left, looking at the Father."

Encarnita goes on: "After taking the photo we went into the dining room of the Villa, which is quite near the gallery. The Father put on his sunglasses to hide his emotion and said he was going to give us his blessing."

The emotion of the founder of Opus Dei is easily understood. They had told him so much about this daughter of his, her fidelity to the spirit of Opus Dei, and her heroism in bearing the sufferings her illness caused. The meeting between the seventeen-year-old girl and Blessed Escrivá must have been very moving and very hard at the same time. God wished to take her so soon! But God knows best.

Encarnita continues: "The Father said he was going to give her his blessing. Montse began to make an effort to kneel down, but the Father did not allow her to. He put his hands on her head and made a sign of the cross on her forehead."

The diary says: "When the Father gave her his blessing he said, 'My daughter, sufferings you have and you will have, but I want you to offer it up for your parents, your brothers and sisters, for the Work, and for me.' "

Later on he said: "Ask our Lord for his will to be done, but that if he wishes you can get well again. Promise me that, from now on, you will always be very faithful."

Encarnita concludes: "When he was leaving, he turned around at the door and stopped for a few seconds, looking at his daughter with immense love and affection."

A letter from Rome

That day she had lunch with the students from the Roman College of Holy Mary and attended the get-together afterwards. "She is always laughing and cheering everyone up," someone wrote in the diary that day. During the reunion, an extensive family gathering, Encarnita sat beside her and told her bits and pieces about the others while they sang songs from different parts of the world.

Like a good Catalan she wished to sing some Catalan songs, helped by Conchita Puig and Teresa Negra. "During the get-together she asked us to sing something in Catalan. I think it was *Muntanyas del Canigó*," recalls Teresa.

While they were singing the others looked at her with a certain sadness, knowing that it was very likely they would never see her again, unless God should work a miracle; even though they tried, they found it difficult to behave as if nothing were the matter. Montse recognized this and tried to pass unnoticed. "Not once did she make a reference to her illness," Manolita Ortíz says.

There was one particularly poignant moment. At the end of a song there were a few seconds when everybody was looking at her in silence. She saved the situation by suggesting they sing a Christmas carol. Christmas was still quite a few weeks away, but what did it matter? They began to sing:

> *My Child, my Child, I am a mule,*
> *But I love you very much.*
> *Child, mount a horse*
> *Let us go along the path,*
> *I will teach you about the earth*
> *You will teach me about Heaven...*

She showed them the present the founder had given her. The diary says: "She was moved showing us the medallion of the Roman College of Our Lady, which the Father gave her this morning. When we saw the image of our Lady, *Regina Operis Dei*, on the reverse side of the medallion we said, commending her, *iter para tutum* – prepare a safe way...."

Pepa continues: "That day, after lunch, they settled her in a room behind the sitting room so that she could rest. She used the time to write to her parents." The first letter was to her mother who had taken the opportunity of her daughter's absence to make a retreat.

Dear Mom,

At the moment I am in the living room of Montagnola. I have already seen the Father.

Well, I am going to explain everything, from the beginning, so you can appreciate what I am experiencing. This morning they came to fetch me by car, as I am not living in Villa Sacchetti. At around eleven I got there and immediately I began to see things, all of them so beautiful! The oratory of the Holy Christ is exquisite; you cannot explain by letter. So I will tell you about it by word of mouth when I get home. The oratory of the Immaculate Heart of Mary is right beside it; it is beautiful too. Then, as soon as I had seen them, Encarnita came down and we went to the sitting room, where the Father received us....

We were there just 2 or 3 minutes when the Father came with Don Alvaro. It was so moving and the Father so simple that this impresses you all the more... He came to me immediately... we sat down and the Father sent someone to fetch Iciar. She came flying. Meantime the Father was asking me about my parents, brothers and sisters, etc. I said you were very well, and when Iciar came, he had us go into a gallery where they took two photographs to send to you. So that Dad will have them by now. What a wonderful detail of affection on the Father's part: don't you think so?

I have interrupted the letter because Encarnita has come up to the sittingroom and we are off with Pepa to see more things, which I will not tell you about. Because, if otherwise, when I return I will have nothing to tell you; and that would never do. As I was saying I am continuing this letter to you after the get-together, which was so wonderful you cannot imagine. Encarnita was there, too, and there were many of us, from many different places. A girl from Venezuela and another from Guatemala played the guitar and the rest of us sang. There was also someone from Peru and very young besides. She is a daughter of the first supernumerary there. We sang lots of familiar songs and very well sung too, as Teresa Negra is the teacher, and she sang divinely. Well, as Encarnita wants to add something, I will say goodbye. Lots of hugs and kisses...

Many women members of Opus Dei from different countries lived in Villa Sacchetti. They had different professions and varied in age, though the majority were under thirty. Some of them, Encarnita Ortega for instance, helped in the governance of the women's section of Opus Dei. Others worked or were studying there while they learned the spirit of the Work from the lips of the founder himself. After living in Rome for a while they would return to their country of origin or go to a new place to begin the Work there. A few stayed on in Italy: Pepa Castelló, for example, who had gone to live in another Center of Opus Dei in Rome on the day before Montse arrived in Italy.

Although Montse lived in Villa delle Palme, Adelaida Sánchez, who at that time lived in Villa Sacchetti, recalls: "She spent quite some time with us.... She was happy with us, as if nothing were the matter. She had difficulty getting around, although she did not attract attention. Only the person who was supporting her by the arm would notice the weight she put on it." During the get-together, Adelaida also recalls, they spoke about the different apostolic enterprises.

"She did not call attention to herself," Adelaida adds, even though the pain was getting worse during her days in Rome. Pepa recalls that "she got much worse during the few days she was in Rome." However, "she bore the pain as well as she could, and would make jokes to conceal the limp."

Pepa reflects that one of Montse's most characteristic traits was to wrap up her pain in cheerfulness. And she made an effort not to talk about herself; she also tried to deny herself, especially in those things that she thought might make other people suffer. Sometimes this made it difficult to realize her sufferings. During Mass she made a special effort not to show her pain: she did not grimace or show any trace of frustration on her face. She stood up, the same as everyone else, when the liturgy required. It was only when she said that it hurt her that they said she should stay seated so that she could follow the Mass in more comfort.

More comfort... up to a point. For when Encarnita asked her if it hurt much, she answered in all simplicity: "Yes. It is as if a mad dog were biting me all the time."

At night that dog seemed to get even more furious. Montse Altozano, regional secretary of Opus Dei in Italy at the time, was worried about her as she thought Montse would not be able to get to sleep because of the pain. "If you wake up tonight with the pain and you can't sleep, come into my room and we'll chat for a while, and then you'll see how well you'll sleep."

"I didn't do it that night," Montse explained, "because I knew she would have to live her normal life the next day...."

That night, when Montse went to bed, she began to feel an agonizing pain. She got up; the pain persisted; she got back into bed. The excruciating pain just went on and on... "I was so exhausted, tossing and turning in bed," she said the next day, "that I got up and danced the *titiritaina* (a popular traditional dance) in front of the image of our Lady. Then, as soon as my head hit the pillow, I fell asleep."

Along the streets of Rome

Next day they went for a short walk in Rome. They looked at the bridges over the Tiber, the Renaissance palaces, the Baroque churches, the Bernini fountains, the old streets with mosaics and images of our Lady on the street corners.... With her image almost everywhere, it was so easy to remember her here, in Rome. It was like a dream for Montse; it was like being in heaven.

And from heaven to earth. Now and again a metallic glint showed among the old Roman cobblestones: a bottle-top. At that time in Spain, children used to play with bottle-tops in the manner of marbles. They filled them with melted wax and zipped them along the wooden or tiled floors. An Italian bottle-top! "Nacho is going to be delighted when he sees them," she thought. She tried to pick them up discreetly from the footpath or beside a table in a restaurant. When she was asked what she was doing, she explained that her brother Ignacio had asked her to bring home Italian bottle-tops for his collection; although he made a concession: "Bring them only if you don't have to bend down." The girl who lived in Villa Sacchetti asked the regular milkman for a good selection of bottle-tops so Montse, happily, was able to take back a bagful for her brother.

The nocturnal pirouette in front of our Lady – the *titiritaina* – and the apparently insignificant bag of bottle-tops, make up a full length portrait of Montse's life. A pain converted into joy, song, dance, music; a little, apparently unimportant, sacrifice that conceals an act of love. These acts of love are, like the bottle-tops, within reach of everybody.... However, she built up a collection.

On one of those days Encarnita was talking to Montse. The founder "had given me the task of speaking to her sensitively and clearly about the possible outcome of her illness, so that she could gain maximum supernatural benefit and be ready to win the final battle. I carried out his wishes as well as I could. She told me she was terrified of physical pain but said 'I think God will give me his grace if I am faithful in doing what he asks of me every day.' Thus I noted that the sense of divine filiation had taken firm root, while she made her fear of pain clear at the same time, in a simple, human way. Her robust piety was evident: devotion to our Lady through the Marian norms of piety, which we live in the Work, and veneration for the Eucharist which she demonstrated by making a proper genuflexion even though it hurt.

"When I saw her cheerfulness, which was obvious at all times – at family get-togethers, in the dining room, etc. I thought that maybe my explanation had not been sufficiently clear. So before she left I asked her if she were ready for whatever might come. She smiled and said she was."

On Sunday, November 16, they went to the Vatican again. Montse was delighted to be near the Pope! They were not able to see him as her trip did not coincide with a papal audience, very infrequent events in those days. Pepa recalls her excitement when she saw the residence of John XXIII, who had already convoked the Ecumenical Council. One of the principal documents of the Council would be promulgated years later. The dogmatic constitution, *Lumen gentium,* proclaimed: "All the faithful of whatever state and condition are called by God, each one according to his own way, to the perfection of holiness with which our heavenly Father is perfect."

With her simple life, Montse was a living example of these teachings, which are rooted in the gospel and which the Council would proclaim to the four corners of the earth. At the age of seventeen, with her time running out, she was incorporating with profound spiritual maturity, and heroically and simply at the same time, this message that the Church proposes for all Christians.

This was the message Blessed Josemaría proclaimed from 1928 onwards. It reminds us that sanctity is within our reach, that each one of us can and ought to be a saint in the midst of the world, in our everyday work, in our own situation. God does not ask us to do extraordinary things to become saints; but rather that we do the ordinary things of each day lovingly, for God. Montse's life was like that, and that was her message – a message of cheerfulness of love of God in little things, joyfully accepting each day's cross. The founder taught: "Our way is one of joy, of loving fidelity to God's service. This joy is not the peal of a silly, purely animal laughter. Our joy has very deep roots; it is something very deep. But it is compatible with physical tiredness, with sorrow..., with difficulties in our interior life and in our apostolic work. Even though at times it seems as if everything is going to collapse, nothing collapses because God does not lose battles. Joy is the result of our divine filiation,

knowing that we are loved by our Father God, who
welcomes us, helps us, and always forgives us."

❀   ❀   ❀

On the plane, on the way home, Montse wrote
a card to Encarnita. *"Fine trip. Everything grand. I
am about to arrive and I am ready for 'everything.'
It is worthwhile. Montse."*

Encarnita said: "The postcard from the plane,
saying she was ready for 'everything' because it is
worthwhile, was her answer to the conversation we
had had."

Lía Vila wrote to Crucita Tabernero on
November 29: "Montse is losing ground with each
passing day. Since her return from Rome she has not
been able to come to Llar a single day. I must say
she is full of good cheer as well as being remarkably
peaceful. They are talking about cutting off her leg,
without any hope of improvement. Both Dr.
Cañadell and her parents are reluctant to go ahead,
and now they are waiting for a prestigious Italian
doctor to see her, although nobody is hopeful of the
outcome.

"It is so sad to see her gradually slipping
away; but with tremendous cheerfulness at the same
time. How wonderfully well she is taking it, her
parents too!"

A spot of madness

As is the custom in so many places in the Catholic world, Llar celebrated the novena to the Immaculate Conception at the beginning of December, building up to the feast itself on December 8. Most of the girls who went to Llar made the novena, and those days were marked by details of love for our Lady.

Rosa recalls: "Montse wished to go to the novena, too, to pray to our Lady. As soon as the official prayers were over, she stayed on in Llar talking to everyone who had come and doing apostolate with them, although she would have been more comfortable at home in bed.... But she thought she had no right to think of herself when there were so many people she could bring to our Lord. She would say: 'This is the push that many girls need and I have to do it.' She thought she had to step up the pace as she had so little time."

Ana María Suriol says: "Her devotion to our Lady I can say was nothing short of madness. That is a fact. Going to Llar every day in her physical state was indeed madness.... She was madly in love. But she went, although at times she would have to lie down on the divan as soon as she arrived. She took off her shoes first of all, even though she was exhausted, so as not to soil the bedspread.... "One of the girls who accompanied her testifies: "She was very careful with the little things, which was quite heroic at times."

A page of the Llar diary tells the story of one of the novena days: "Montse came and lay down on the bed for a while.... From her bed she sang with all the rest.... They are very impressed by her cheerfulness. Quite a few of them come to us to ask: 'Is it true that Montse is so ill, she seems so happy!?' Of course she is. Her disposition is marvelous. She wants to give whatever our Lord asks."

"Lots of girls came to the novena," Rosa says, " as many as, fifty or sixty. The oratory was packed. I remember Montse was sitting one day with her leg resting on a chair, as she could not bend it, and she was more comfortable like that. She did her best, as always, not to attract attention."

The priest began the meditation. The only lights were those spotlighting the tabernacle and a small lamp on the priest's table, so that the oratory was in semi-darkness to facilitate personal prayer with our Lord.

"At that moment," Rosa relates, "a girl came into the oratory, and in the half-light she did not notice that Montse was resting her leg on the chair. She asked, 'Is this chair free?' Montse smiled and answered: 'Yes, of course. Sit down please...' and removed her leg, giving up the chair, so the girl never noticed.

"I was upset when I saw what had happened and I came up behind her as best I could, and whispered – because we were in the oratory – would she please prop her leg on my chair.

'If you get up,' she said pulling a face, so that

I would sit down, 'I will be cross with you for the rest of my life.'

"So I had to go and sit down. Besides, I myself was not in very good physical shape either to be standing up the whole time...."

8

Christmas Night

After the novena she spent more time in bed and she prayed, sang and talked with those who came to visit her during those days. Now and again they would play parcheesi or some other game.

Rosa recalls Montse winning sometimes... but then other times she did not. Rosa never saw her sufficiently unhappy to let her win. "We used to play such games with all the enthusiasm in the world. And when I did badly... she was delighted!

"Strange, isn't it? How well I remember those light-hearted occasions! It is understandable. We were so young, so vibrantly young....

"Still I admire her most when I think of these silly things, because I appreciate how she was able to combine suffering with cheerfulness. At her side I understood, with a new insight, the words of the

founder of Opus Dei: 'sadness is the dross of ego-
ism.' She said: 'Yes, it's like that... but there are
worse things.' True, the only real misfortune is sin. I
realized she made an effort to smile when she was
with me so that I would not worry."

Rosa could not believe it.... How could she
possibly have changed so much in such a short time?
Later on she realized it was the work of the Holy
Spirit, the love of God that was taking over her soul
as she corresponded to his grace.... However, she
was surprised when, for an instance, someone as
impatient as Montse sometimes was, could acquire
such resignation, and, in spite of a lot of suffering,
never behave like a chronic invalid. She did not give
way to self-pity. Nor did she like people to pity her,
or to say, "Poor Montse." It was thanks to the sacraments, to prayer, to her relationship with God... and
to something else that had a tremendous impact:
meeting the Father in Rome. She was helped enormously by what he said to her.

There is nothing to compare...

You could hear the first Christmas carols just
beginning on the radio. Christmas was fast
approaching. Ana María and other friends began to
decorate Montse's room, already festooned with
flags. From her bed Montse directed operations: "the
blue star over there; the advent wreath on the lamp;
leave some space over there for the Christmas cards,

so we can put them up as they come." She also had a ceramic plaque with an incisive motto: "Always cheerful."

Rosa continues: "I remember that Fr. Vall, a priest of Opus Dei, used to attend her there. He was rather formal. One day the door was half open and suddenly Montse said: 'Hey Rosa, come here quickly; look Fr. Vall is taking Rafaelito for a walk....' I peeped out quietly, and there he was in the corridor, playing with the baby....

"These incidents struck her. 'The people of Opus Dei are so good,' she said. 'Aren't we lucky?'

"It made me think.... I understood what it was she meant: that it is great luck to have a vocation, a special grace from God, for which we must be eternally grateful. Our founder would say to us that Jesus Christ had called us from all eternity, that he had kissed our foreheads; that is what vocation is, an undeserved gift, the good fortune to walk very near our Lord, following his steps. That is why I think he loved this Christmas carol:

There is nothing to compare with looking for Christ,
There is nothing to compare with looking for Christ,
There is nothing to compare..."

Rosa particularly recalls Montse's struggle in little things during that time, her constant effort not to give other people problems. She continues: "If you are different because of a physical problem, no matter what kind, as was our case... well, you have to try to adapt to others, and not expect them to adapt to you. We used to talk a lot about this. It is we who have to reach out to others rather than wait for them to come to us."

Her family helped enormously. "Especially her parents," Rosa says. "What sacrifices they made to give her everything she looked forward to having!

"I remember one day her father managed to borrow a car, because he wished Montse to see the streets of Barcelona, all illuminated with Christmas lights.

"She was all set to go out. But when the moment came to go to the car she could not, because she had an onset of acute pain.

"And then... everybody reacted as if nothing untoward had happened. She concealed the pain as well as she could, while her parents said: 'Don't worry, it doesn't matter, Montse. So what! We'll send the car back right now. Don't you worry about it....' There was always an atmosphere of cordial relationships and cheerfulness."

A bright and cheerful home

"What an affectionate household," Rosa continues. "It really was one of those 'bright and cheerful homes' the Father used to talk about. They never said 'My God, what a burden we have to carry' or 'What a disaster has come upon this house' or anything of the sort. Quite the contrary; whenever I went to visit Montse, instead of talking to me about her sorrow, she would ask me how I was, how my parents were, if my mother were well, if I liked the lectures I attended at the University, and which subject I was finding more difficult. Clearly they were all so close to our Lord that you could feel the presence of God through their behavior.... One can smile fairly easily for one day. But to keep it up day in and day out... always with the same disposition... with the same affection all the time, the same warmth...."

Rosa continues: "I remember that when Montse's pain became unbearable and she could no longer cope, her mother would ask us to leave the room and she would stay behind consoling her:

'Montse, Montse, you'll see how it will soon go.... My darling, you must complain; if you do, we can help you better...'

'No,' Montse would say, with tears in her eyes, 'don't worry, Mom, I am fine now, much better.'

"The atmosphere in the house was neither dramatic, nor tense nor depressed. If it were, I would not have been able to bear it....

"It is strange. In spite of everything that was happening, I remember there was a very pleasant atmosphere in the house, especially over the Christmas period."

The first anniversary

It was to be her last Christmas on earth and Montse knew it; she also knew it would be very different from every previous Christmas. She would not be able to go with her mother, brothers, and sisters to the cathedral square as she had done in other years, to look for a new figure for the Crib amongst the knickknacks of the outdoor stalls. A year ago, to the day, she had been to this market with Pepa. And just a few hours later she had written the letter asking for admission to Opus Dei, giving herself to God completely. She rang up Rosa, absolutely thrilled to tell her.

"Rosa, it's my anniversary!"

It was only one year ago and how things had changed! You could not hear the childrens' squeals of joy in the corridor at the start of the holidays. Everybody tried to be quiet so as not to disturb Montse. Lía says: "One afternoon I was there with her and her parents, in silence. The room was in semi-darkness with the shutters practically closed. Suddenly Montse exclaimed:

'Put the lights on! Open the shutters! Stop whispering! Why don't we sing a song? A Christmas carol?'

"She wanted us to be cheerful... and we began to sing her favorite carol."

Child, mount a horse
Let us go along the path,
I will teach you about the earth
You will teach me about Heaven...

The Russian treatment

Montse's parents had hoped to take her to Llar, thinking Montse would like to celebrate Christmas Eve there. However, the pain got steadily worse as the day went by and the inflammation in her leg increased. Montse tried to play it down. Her father recalls: "It was precisely on the 24th that we received some pills from Russia that we had been expecting since August. We had got them through our Belgian ambassador. The secretary of the Belgian Embassy in Moscow had come to Barcelona for Christmas and she brought them. I had read about them in a medical magazine, and I was very hopeful as they almost guaranteed a cure."

Dr. Cañadell was consulted. He recalls: "Naturally, her father was prepared to do anything that might give hope of saving Montse's life. On more than one occasion he had suggested amputating her leg, but I had explained that, in her case, amputation would not solve anything. I only considered it to be useful if her leg swelled so much that it became too heavy and the pain unbearable.

"Then her father read, in a medical publication, about the Russians experimenting with a drug called sarcolisina and he managed to get some, after moving heaven and earth…. He had great faith in the sarcolisina; I am afraid I did not. It was in the purely experimental stage. But we decided to do everything that we could for Montse and we began to administer these pills…."

With the doctor's approval, what was the best thing to do? Give them to her immediately, on such a special day? Why not wait a day or two? Still, they thought, the sooner the treatment was started, the better.

They made up their minds to let Montse herself decide. Yes that would be the best thing to do.

"Montse," her mother asked her, "what do you think? Should you take the pills today or wait until tomorrow?"

She replied with her usual serenity: "Whatever you think best." Dr. Cañadell said: "Although Montse was very keen to go to midnight Mass and was aware that the medicine might make her sick, she took it. She showed herself to be prudent and wise. She had what we call in Catalonia a *gran seny*, great savvy."

Her mother explains. "We could see how her illness progressed, and we were anxious to begin treatment as soon as possible. She never refused any treatment, no matter how painful. She never asked, 'Why are you doing this to me? What is this medicine for?' So we decided she should take these pills immediately, even though they might provoke some reaction...."

"Some reaction!" her mother comments. "Those pills were terrible. Every time she took one she spent from six to eight hours vomiting and feeling really awful.

"We could not go to Llar, despite her longing. We spent the whole night with her in this distressing

way. The three youngest, Pili, María Jose, and Crucina, and of course Rosario – actually Pili was quite a
bit older but she was part of the choir – sang Christmas carols for her, during the moments of relative
calm.

"Suddenly we would have to stop singing
because she was feeling bad again and began to
vomit. When she recovered we went on. But half
way through the carol she began to feel bad, and
again more vomiting. When she was better, we
carried on.

"It was already the small hours when she
could at last get some rest…. That is how she spent
her last Christmas Eve at home."

Joy and sorrow

There was a repeat performance, Christmas
carols and vomiting, on New Year's Eve, with her
leg ever more inflamed, while the noisy celebration
of the arrival of 1959 in the streets of Barcelona
reached her bedroom.

Lía wrote to the founder: "Happy New Year!
We prayed intensely for you on the ninth and our
Lord rewarded us with a new vocation on that day.
For some time now, in Llar, our Lord has been
blessing us constantly…. We are convinced that
Montsita's sufferings have great value before our
Lord. You cannot imagine, Father, how impressed
all the girls are. She is in such good humor that she

encourages everybody. She has some very bad moments, but she endures them cheerfully and optimistically."

Dr. Cañadell made another visit. He recalls: "As I said before, I had no faith in the sarcolisina. But we wished to leave no stone unturned. However, when we saw that each pill caused such anguish, I said: 'Look Montse, if it makes you feel so ill, what do you think about giving it up?'

"She replied: 'Don't ask me what I think, just say if I should take them or not...'

"I advised her to stop."

María del Carmen Delclaux says: "Even though she felt quite bad, as she knew how to knit and so did I, she suggested making a garment for Lía as a present from the Three Kings for January 6. I told her not to worry, being ill as she was; but she insisted so much that I finally gave in. I remember her there, knitting in bed, lying quite flat, because she could not sit up, making a huge effort. But she was so happy doing it!"

She wanted everybody to be happy. Sometimes she would hum a tune or ask people to sing. It was not always easy. There were times when they did not feel able. On one occasion when she asked them to sing, her mother broke into song immediately, but her father with tears in his eyes pretended to be reading the paper. Montse realized what was happening and said to him: "Dad, I can't hear you... I want you to be cheerful."

One of her big preoccupations was that no one

should suffer for her. One day she called her father and asked him: "Dad, are you happy?" She did the same with each member of the family. She added, "We are the happiest family in Barcelona. When I die I don't want anyone to be sad: You must be cheerful."

"She would forget about herself and her ordeal completely to cheer up others," comments one of the girls who went to Llar. "One afternoon I found her a bit more washed out than usual when I arrived; so in my efforts to cheer her up I told her an amusing story I had seen on television She enjoyed it a lot, and later on, when others of the Work came, she got me to tell it again, for them to share in the entertainment. Later on, I heard that she told Lía how that afternoon her leg hurt a lot and she felt sick, but she did not complain so as not to spoil the enjoyment for others."

"This was one of the things that most impressed me about her," María del Carmen says. "She would become so absorbed with others, it was hard to know if she was in pain or not. I recall arriving at her house one day and finding her cousins and friends from Seva there, telling her amusing stories. Her mother took me aside before going in and said:

'Look here, I think Montse is not well at all just now. You go in and if you see she is suffering, cut the visit short and tell everyone to go.'

"I went in. She appeared so excited, talking to the others, going over the summer events in Seva, the play they put on, that I said nothing until the girls themselves got up to leave. Then, just as they were going out and closing the door, she exclaimed. 'I can't go on, I can't go on any longer.' And she threw off the blankets as she could not stand the weight over her leg. I called her mother at once and we calmed her down as best we would. She was enduring intense pain, a pain that a few minutes ago you could not even notice..."

"Living for others" inspired Montse not to retreat into her distress but to give herself to others even in the smallest things. Some afternoons the pain would ease a little and they would take her to Llar. She never forgot about others during these coming and goings. She said to María del Carmen: "I have seen a lovely jacket that would suit you. You must go and see it."

Her cheerfulness was infectious. Dr. Cañadell says: "I never saw her sad or embittered or over-whelmed. All my visits to her were of a lively, cheerful, animated nature, with never a sign of sadness despite the gravity of her illness...."

This makes her suffer

From mid-January on, dressing Montse's leg became more and more painful. "Her leg was so tremendously inflamed," María del Carmen recalls, "when I was helping to take care of her, it weighed so much that sometimes, as I was unable to hold it up, I had to kneel on the floor so she could rest it on my shoulder."

"The inflammation was such that her leg had a circumference of 60 cm," Rosa says. "Until one day... the inflammation burst. When it came to dressing it, the smell was awful, which caused her immense suffering, as she suffered for us. She always suffered for others....

"I am overcome by the memory of it, but at the time I was pretty concerned. For when we were alone and the pain became strong, the poor darling would cry, clench her fists and say she thought she could not stand any more pain.... Later on she would ask me to forgive her:

'Rosa, what a coward I am! Honestly, I am ashamed of myself...'

'What nonsense!' I would reply. 'You are so brave.... Besides, you need to complain, because complaining relieves the tension....'

"However, when Dr. Cañadell came and inquired:

'Montse, how are you? Have you had a good afternoon?' she would invariably reply:

'Fine.'

'How can you say 'Fine'? Don't you remember what you have been through? You have had the most frightful pains!'

"She would pinch me, without the doctor noticing, for me to shut up. As soon as he had left she would say:

'But Rosa what is the point of telling him? Dr. Cañadell does all he can... He can't do any more.

And that makes him sad...."'

"She was always very humble," Fr. Manuel Vall adds. "She never thought she was bearing her illness well: she thought she was very faint-hearted and complained too much...."

"Then when she had a respite," Rosa goes on, "she would pretend to pick a quarrel with me. I was studying pharmacy and she would say, jokingly, that all the medicines that I brought her were no good. 'You see, they are no good for anything.'

"I would go to the pharmaceutical laboratories with a sensation of complete impotence, on seeing a girl of seventeen lying dying and there was no medicine to cure her. I would say to the people there:

'All these things you sell are no use for anything! Anything at all! You are not even able to invent a medicine to cure this illness!' "

Manolita recalls: "It would take four of us to do the dressing. Two would hold up her leg, another would apply gauze, while I would be putting on the bandage almost simultaneously. We did it as fast as we could; even so, the operation lasted quite a while. And when we had removed the bandage of the previous day, sometimes it was not just skin that came off with it...."

Teresa González and María Gambús usually formed part of this team. María Gambús recalls the dressing "became more and more painful and delicate, because of the amount of ulcers she was developing." "Other times," her mother continues, "we would cause a small hemorrhage. There was a constant foul smell. It was noticeable only when the leg was uncovered; besides, we had three jars of air-purifiers dotted around the room. The four of us who did the dressings had a really bad time. Sometimes we thought we would not be able to stand it....

"When I describe these things, there is always someone who says: 'Really, Manolita, I don't see how you could stand it....' I just reply: 'Look, you are making a big mistake if you think there was any merit on my part. I can assure you there was none. What there really was, was great grace, a great assistance from our Lord. That is why if something similar were to happen to you, you wouldn't have to worry. God will help you and give you the help that you don't have now because you don't need it.'

"Besides, God fits the back for the burden.... With the one hand he takes away and with the other he provides, because he doesn't want you to go mad with pain... because life must go on and you have eight other children and you have to keep up the fight.'

"When I think back to those months now I find it is almost impossible that Manuel and I were able to endure it. More than once I have asked myself: 'You were able to do all this?' I always reply to myself, 'No.'

"That is the truth. We really did not do it ourselves. God helped us and he gave us an extraordinary grace not to die of sorrow and pity seeing her like that....

"That is why there are some things which,

when I remember them, seem to me to be almost un-real.... But they were true. I would take off her bandage with total calm. There was a tremendous stench! On removing the bandage, bits of flesh would come off with it... and I washed it... and then I sat down at the table and ate some food as if nothing had happened. I even put some weight on.

"Then I would sit by her side and we would pray... I could see our Lord there. No visions though! I just felt his presence, there, in my daughter who was dying....When I could no longer cope as I was on the point of busting into tears, I would go outside, or I would go to a nearby church to calm down and then, quite peacefully, I would go home. Because, you see, I could not cry at home...."

Painkillers

"However, she did not complain," Rosa continues, "and she took everything they gave her except for the painkillers, she was reluctant to take them...."

"Yes," her mother confirmed. "I remember us saying to her to take cibalgina, a relatively mild sedative, and she would resist." Dr. Cañadell recalls this too.

"I did not understand her resistance at all at the time," Rosa continues. "I realize now she was afraid the painkillers would make her sleep and diminish her capacity to do apostolate. That is a fact, sedatives do make you sleepy. One day I said, "Take them, you will be more relaxed and you will sleep better...." Maybe that was my mistake.... I am not sure, but I have always suspected she did not take them for that reason: they would interfere with her apostolate, with talking about God with her friends. I would insist: 'Take them, they will lessen the pain.' She would reply: 'Definitely not. They will make me sleepy.'

"She told Lía quite clearly that if she took them she would not be able to offer her sufferings to our Lord, for the Pope, for Opus Dei, and for the Father.

"Besides she did not wish her parents to spend money on her. 'I am the eldest,' she would say 'and just imagine the expense I am causing them.'

"Some afternoons, when I went to visit, her mother would go out to fetch the children from school and we were left alone. Then she would tell me lots of things... we were very close to each other....

"If the pain in her leg became acute, she would endure the pain as well as she could. 'I can't, I can't, carcinoma is so very painful.... Rosa please, let us do the prayer....'

"We made the sign of the Cross and I would begin with the introductory prayer: 'My Lord and my God, I firmly believe that you are here, that you see me, that you hear me. I adore you with profound reverence. I ask you for pardon of my sins, and grace to make this time of prayer fruitful. My

Mother Immaculate, St. Joseph my father and lord, my guardian angel, intercede for me....'

"We began the prayer in silence and Montse would stay very, very still, praying, bottling up the pain....

"Her mother, however, as soon as she came in and looked at her, realized immediately everything that had happened....

"I have already said we were very close. I believe this for two reasons. First of all, being a pharmacist, I understood her pain very well. Secondly, because I was in a somewhat similar situation, the one who can best understand others is one suffering a similar situation. However, seeing the state she was in, compared to me, I would say:

'Montse, you can't compare....'

'Yes but look. You have to walk like that...'

'True, I cannot move about easily, nor can I go skiing or on a picnic.... 'But you have to realize that I have no pain whatsoever.... If I did!!? Why, as soon as I have the slightest headache, I rush off to take some aspirins!'

"So that people would to go confession, so that her friends got closer to God... nothing was too much. Besides, she would do it with such flair when they came to see her and would inquire:

'Montse, how are you?'

She replied invariably: 'Fine!'

'Can I do anything for you?'

'Not really... well... would you like to do something that would make me really, really happy?'

'Yes, of course, What?'

'Well look here... there is a retreat... if you were to go... you would make me so very happy...'

"And then, with her big smile, so cheerful, she would tell jokes and she would laugh and sing the song that I was teaching her to play on the guitar....

"Really I have never understood how it occurred to me to teach her to play the guitar at that time, when I knew she was dying. Later on I have pondered on these things, and I still do not understand them. The joy I had when I arrived at her house and the joy I had on leaving it... horrible as it was from a human point of view... I could not tell anyone about these things because no one understood; no one could understand an atmosphere of such cheerfulness..."

Six chords

"It became more difficult for her to eat," María Gambús recalls, "and we would encourage her, asking her to offer up each spoonful to our Lord."

"Won't you try this, Montsina?" her mother said on one occasion, "for what, you already know...." Montse said she would, and she had a little soup and then some more. But suddenly she threw it all up, showing that she had had a very bad moment. Then she lifted up her eyes to heaven and said:

'Lord, why did it have to happen right now?' as if to
say, 'But I was offering it up to you….'

"Later on, when she was feeling better, she
asked us to sing," Rosa continues. "There was a
particular song she liked a lot.

> *I remember the time I met you*
> *I remember the afternoon*
> *But I don't remember how I saw you*
> *And I will tell you that I fell in love...*

"When we got to the phrase, '*A soul to con-
quer you: a heart to love you,*' she whispered:
'Rosa: Capital letter. Capital letter...' so we would
sing it with reference to God, as the Father had
taught us. We carried on:

> *A soul to conquer You:*
> *A heart to love You,*
> *A life to live beside You...*

"*A life to live beside You...* She said she would
like to be able to accompany all these songs with the
guitar. There were just six chords! I thought she
would not be able to achieve it as it is very difficult
to learn to play the guitar in bed.... However, in spite
of what I thought, she did learn. She teased me about
this.

'I learned didn't I?' she said.

'Of course,' I replied. 'But that's because you
have such a magnificent teacher.'

'You? Ha ha! You only know six chords!' (In fact, I did only know six chords!)

That is how she was, very natural and spontaneous. She had no guile. She never gave me any soft soap... not once! She never flattered me. She did not say, 'Oh yes, Rosa, you have taught me so well!'

"No, she never said anything to make me blush or feel embarrassed. On the contrary: she teased me. 'Rosa, is that all you know? Do you only know six chords?' Then I would pretend to be cross:

'Well, madam, maybe I only know six... but I have taught you how to play them!'

"The fact is that she learned very quickly. She was a star pupil. I didn't tell her that either; on the contrary, whenever she made a mistake I would come down on her: 'now, my girl, do it again.... Are you stupid?'

"And we went on like this enjoying ourselves hugely. I think about it now, and it seems impossible. I really do not know how I was able to spend so many tough moments by her side and yet we were, both of us, so happy. Maybe it is that beside her I learned, by her example, what our founder has taught us: what really makes a person miserable is to try to banish the cross from her own life; that meeting the cross is meeting Christ, Love itself....

"Beside her I learned how to love.... I know that is not the right word, but there is no other; but I learned how to love her illness, and my own.

"She was sorry she was not able to get up to help me walk.... She would say: 'Look, Rosa! Everybody helps you very well, fantastically well: they all do it lovingly, but I used to enjoy helping you.'"

Amidst songs and laughter

María del Carmen says: "Montse did not want to be the cause of our wasting time. She knew I had a lot of study to do; so when I visited her, she would make me study…. She herself did not waste time. She wished to use it as well as possible to do apostolate….

"In January she came to Llar just a few times. Sometimes she was so weak, she hardly had the strength to dress herself; but she wanted us to take her to Llar. We would put a long coat on top of her clothes, fetch a taxi, take her to Llar, and settle her on the sofa in the sitting room. There she would see all her friends and talk to them about God."

It was a vibrant, youthful, and profoundly cheerful apostolate. Ana María Suriol relates: "The first thing she did was to sing, accompanying herself on the guitar... She did this to avoid us talking about her or concentrating on her. In a word, she tried to conceal her pain and her illness as far as possible."

On other days she was not well enough to go out, so she used the occasion to talk about God with the friends who came to visit her. But, as the founder of Opus Dei had taught her, prayer and mortification prepared the terrain. Fr. Manuel Vall, the priest who attended to Montse spiritually, said "from her bed,

Montse did a lot of apostolate with her prayer."

In spite of the pain, she was happy. Although, on some mornings when the windows were opened and the street noise entered her room bathed in light, she could not help feeling some sadness. Outside, life was vibrant and pulsating with all its strength, while hers was ebbing.... For a few brief seconds she felt how much she was leaving behind.

Rosa continues: "There was another song she loved, which she would usually sing in a loud voice, with all the exuberance of youth:

> *On the faraway mountain*
> *The horseman is riding*
> *He roams the world alone*

Longing for death

"During this time I think she accepted death with all her heart, though she did not seek it. She desired to live; she wanted to live with all her might. Later on, she lost even this desire; in the last few months she was burning with the desire to meet with God and she spoke of death as an embrace with Love. The only thing she was horrified of was the coffin....

"She thought more frequently about heaven.... I encouraged her to go on living, and every time a new medicine appeared, like injections of a pyeanese antibiotic, I would say:

'Look Montse! It says here that there have been fabulous results.... You'll see how great this medicine is. This is it!' "

❀   ❀   ❀

Montse's mother says: "From my point of view I never noticed Montse giving the slightest attention to her medication. Every morning I would distribute the pills, and she never said, 'Mom, remember to give me such and such a pill, it is over-due....' Not once! She always took them automatically, with total indifference.... She never asked, 'Mom, let us make a novena for me to get better.' Not at all! Neither did she complain about her situation; not ever."

"That is a fact," her father agrees. "The only pills she found especially difficult to take were the Russian ones, which caused terrible vomiting... but in the end she took them."

"One day," Rosa says, "when I arrived she said:

'I have been thinking a lot today....'

'Yes, what about?'

'I was thinking that ... I am going to say to our Lord that you should die too.'

'Good Lord...! What on earth makes you say

that?' I answered her, absolutely furious.

'It is just that I thought you must be fed up with walking like that, and maybe you would like to be with our Lord soon....'

"She really upset me. I told her she was very well prepared to get to heaven, but that I was not. Later on I said more light-heartedly.

'Besides, imagine that instead of going to heaven like you... I were to be sent some other place, limbo, for instance!'

"She laughed. However, from that moment on, I appreciated her more and understood her distress better; I realized how much I loved life and how wonderful life is.

"The truth is I did not have, nor do I have, any desire whatsoever to die... I also said I would not go home until she gave up praying for it.... Then she said that I should not worry, she would stop. And so she would, because she was very sincere. When she said something, she meant it....

"In any case, I was intrigued. Did she want to die or did she not? We only talked about it once. Just the one time.

"It was ages afterwards when I said to her:

'Montse, how on earth did it occur to you to pray for that, when I have no desire whatsoever to die? Do you not want to keep on living?'

"Then she said in all simplicity:

'Look Rosa, if a new medicine comes out I will take it; if they have to cut my leg off, let them. If our Lord wants me to die, I will die. I try to survive because I am a member of Opus Dei, because I want to serve our Lord, because I would like to avoid my parents suffering. I love life... but if God wants me to die, I will die.... because I can also help from heaven.'

"And we never talked about it again."

❀   ❀   ❀

9

I want to see your face, Lord

Montse loved life, as life is a gift from God.
She accepted death, if that were God's will, with the
same joy. She wanted to live and die at the same
time: ultimately, she wanted to do God's will. She
thought of God as a loving father, who always
wanted what was best – even though, so often, it was
incomprehensible from a human point of view. She
accepted life or death peacefully, calmly, with a
smile on her face. If God is total happiness and this
happiness is forever, why should she be sad? She
even had time for make-up!

In spite of her situation she never abandoned
her outward appearance. "She brushed her teeth,"
her father notes, "right up to the last day."

Those who took care of her were surprised,
but there was nothing to be surprised about: it was

one of those little ways she showed her consideration for others. Hadn't she learned to play the guitar
to cheer up everyone around her during that difficult
time? Taking care of her appearance was a small but
important sign of consideration for others; because
nothing is more upsetting than to see someone lan-
guishing in bed, looking a mess, so often an obvious
sign of having given up, of despair, of 'what's the
use…?'

"Sometimes," Carmen Salgado recalls, "we
would say to her when we arrived: 'Montse, how
very pretty you look today!' And she would answer
amusedly:

'I have smartened myself up to be ready for
you!"

However, for all her efforts to cover up, her
state of health was obviously getting worse. She had
almost completely lost her appetite and, day after
day, it was the same sad story.

"Montse won't you have a little more?... This
is really delicious..."

In the end, to get her to take anything at all,
they used the ultimate resort.

"Montse, come on. Look here, offer this up
for a vocation."

Then she would take it, even though each
spoonful was a real torment. She never asked for any
particular food.

The time came when she could only take hot
chocolate. Carmen Salgado says: "As they could not
get it in the local shops, I would bring it. But she did

not want to be a nuisance to me. 'Have you had to come just for this?' she would ask. I always made out it was not just for that, so she would not suspect I had gone especially to buy it."

A novena to Isidoro

Meanwhile everyone was praying for her cure and the family was praying through the intercession of Isidoro Zorzano. They would read aloud from his prayer card:

"O God who filled your Servant Isidoro with so many treasures of your grace in the fulfillment of his professional duties in the midst of the world: help me to know also how to sanctify my ordinary work and to be an apostle to my friends and companions...."

Isidoro and Montse: two members of Opus Dei whose causes of beatification have been opened by the Church; two members of very different mentality, circumstances, personality, and nationality, but united in the same desire for holiness, having the self-same vocation. Isidoro is an admirable example of fidelity to his vocation and the sanctification of everyday work done for the love of God. She had to be a saint too, like Isidoro, in her work, her illness. This was "her Opus Dei," which she had to convert into God's work.

❀   ❀   ❀

What a paradox! Everyone was praying for her "to stay"; she however desired "to go," though she did not say it as not to sadden them. Until one day she inquired:

"What are you asking for me?"

"Whatever is best for you."

"Aren't you asking for me to go soon?"

"No, Montse, we could not ask for that."

"It's just that... I want to go."

"Yes, but when God wills..."

She became silent and then said:

"Okay."

"Okay..." That one word meant a total acceptance of God's will; the familiar version of an aspiration that she often repeated: "Lord, whenever you want it, however you want it, and wherever you want it."

I will never leave you

"Darling, I love talking to you about heaven," her mother said to her one day, "so that I can see you smile."

That was a fact. She felt happy thinking that heaven was getting nearer all the time. She told everyone: friends, brothers, sisters, and Lía:

"No one would believe it, but I am really happy."

"Well, Montse," Lía encouraged her, " a little bit more patience and then you'll be having a good time forever."

Forever! This word reminds us of Teresa of Avila who encouraged her brother, when they escaped through the Adaja Gate "to be beheaded by the Moors"; forever! It inspired and reassured her.

"Jorge, do you realize," she told her brother, "happy forever? Don't you forget it, forever!"

It was not a selfish "forever." "I assure you," she repeated, "that from heaven I will help you a lot. I will never leave you."

But they reminded her that on earth she could do such a lot! This certainly inspired in her "that thirst to suffer," proper to saintly souls, as well as a filial trust based on the thought that if God gave her the burden he would also give her the strength to carry it...

"In that sense nothing could shake her," Rosa continues. "She did not worry about her illness. She was always thinking about the apostolate; that is why she missed not being able to go to Llar more often – she could not attend the meditations given by the priest, she was not able to be with the girls, or do apostolate with them...."

"I would say to her: 'Think about yourself and about your leg.' But she took no notice of me. She wanted to go on... on the attack.

"That is how she was right up to the last minute, on the attack. She never struck her colors. She never gave in... Right up to the end she was praying, struggling, laughing...."

When I was by her side

Rosa says: "In a very short time she matured both from a human and a spiritual point of view. She had a very rich interior life. I noticed it all the time. To such an extent during the last month of her life, that I wrote down everything she said, and when I got home I would take it to prayer because these things helped me a lot in my own relationship with our Lord....

"I was older than she was, both in age and in the length of time we belonged to Opus Dei. So at the beginning I considered myself better 'prepared' than she was. Can you imagine?... Until I realized that Montse had a deep intimacy with our Lord... However, she continued to be the same Montse as always; she was never overbearing, you never felt uncomfortable at her side. I never felt overwhelmed by her interior life; on the contrary, she communicated her love for God to me. At her side I could tell she was really very close to God and this brought me closer to him.... It was something similar to what had happened to me when I met the Father for the first time....

"It is very important for me to have known her. I understood why God had given me my illness, and why he gave me the grace to know someone like her, which was how I always thought people of Opus Dei should be.... She was so normal and so supernatural at the same time, combining both aspects so gracefully.... Her unity of life was remarkable.... Actually human life and spiritual life were not two facets for her, but just one, but so tightly entwined you did not know which one it was....

"I hardly know how to explain it. Her words helped me to pray more than a meditation or a sermon by the priest did.... When I heard her say the introductory prayer, 'My Lord and my God, I firmly believe that you are here, that you see me, that you hear me...', I was certain that God was there with us, that he saw us and heard us...."

The dressings

One sleepless night followed another; long, painful nights when Montse used to offer up her pain for different people. And daytime brought the dressings which, Carmiña recalls, she offered up for a specific intention: the Church, the Pope, priests. "The first dressing of the day, the worst one, Carmiña says, "she would always offer up for the founder of Opus Dei and everyone who lived with him in Rome."

As her illness got worse, the dressings became more painful and complicated, "a nurse, a friend of her mother, came to do the dressings," Carmiña recalls, "and her father got her up from the bed, holding her with both arms in the air, while she sang: 'Tachin, tachin, tachin!' to defuse the situation. Meanwhile, they would change the sodden sheets caused by seepage from her leg... until she would say: 'I can't take it any more,' and we would lay her down and let her be still....

"In addition we had to massage the other leg, so it would not get pins and needles in it, or get stiff from lack of use. But the time came when we could not touch her bad leg without causing her tremendous pain. They had to build a cage so that the sheets would not touch it. Every time we did the dressing we would apply a towel to absorb the liquid that oozed out of the wound."

"What a wound! What a smell!" Enrique recalls, "and she was so sensitive...! She was not a flirt, but she was very feminine. Of course, her sensibility rebelled against these unpleasant aspects of her illness. However, she endured it all with incredible patience... when precisely impatience had been one of her main characteristics!

"How she had changed! When she was little, she wanted everything right away! And she got irritated if things did not turn out as she had foreseen. So she got upset. On the other hand, now..."

❀   ❀   ❀

Her friends would give her intentions to pray for: someone who could have a vocation, a sick person.... On one occasion she said, "I love the sick very specially." She felt particularly close to them because of their suffering.

Other pain she would offer up for the Church, the Pope, for the apostolate of Opus Dei in Paris where she would now not be able to go, for her friends in Llar…. One day, as soon as she woke up, the first thing she asked her mother was how many girls had asked for admission to Opus Dei in Llar recently.

"Eleven. Why do you ask?"

"Well last night as I could not sleep, I was praying for them one by one, but I could only count ten. I will have to offer up lots of things this morning for the one I left out, because the poor thing has had none."

❀   ❀   ❀

She asked all of us to help her in her struggle. Pilar Martin recalls: "Her parents helped her with unbounded generosity in what our Lord required of them, lovingly, tirelessly, never yielding in what ought to be done."

Dr. Cañadell states: "In my opinion, her parents had two different, complementary attitudes towards her illness. Her mother never thought Montse would get better, so she helped Montse to abandon herself in God's hands and did everything possible for her to make use of the pain to get closer to God and to bring many others to God also. Her father believed she would be cured and used all the means possible to disprove the doctor's prognosis.

They are not two opposing positions: they were very united. It does not mean that Manolita did not use all possible human means for her cure or that Manuel did not abandon himself to God's will, which I always saw him do. What I want to point out is that each one put their own stamp on their way of acting, both ways being deeply and faultlessly Christian."

"The whole atmosphere surrounding Montse was supportive," says Rosa, "very supernatural and very normal at the same time! When the youngest one of three, maybe four, would come home from school, his mother would say: 'Quiet, we mustn't bother Montse.' I could hear him play with his car in the corridor, 'brum… brum… brum…' under his breath, while he pushed it up and down... You could hear a pin drop. Everybody took such care….

"But nobody was embittered or upset; her parents had the same good humor as always! Her mother was so gentle, so loving towards her, with me too, with everyone…. This helped Montse to keep up the struggle right to the end."

❀   ❀   ❀

The words she had heard from the lips of the founder in Rome were her basic strength, inspiring and encouraging her in the day-to-day struggle. Hanging in her room she had the photo Helena Serrano had taken of her meeting with the Father in Rome. Encarnita Ortega tells how "it served as a source of encouragement and strength during her illness; she had it hanging up in front of her and it reminded her to commend the intentions of the founder of the Work." But would she be able to stick it out until the end? She needed the help of everyone's prayers. With the help of her mother she wrote to Encarnita:

My dear Encarnita,

I am having a tough time and I rely on your help, which I really need, during this long protracted end. I am not forgetting you, nor will I. Best wishes and all my love.

Montse

Lía wrote to the founder on February 1: "With each passing day we realize the value of the apostolate of suffering. Montse is bearing up wonderfully well, enduring everything with great peace and joy. She has had the courage to come to lunch twice this week and then she stayed on until nighttime. Coming and going are a real torture for her, but the distraction makes it worthwhile. However, we believe she won't be able to do it much more; those of us who see her every day can notice a steady deterioration, but she maintains a tremendous interest in everything and prays for everything by offering up her sufferings."

Because of her worsening condition Montse, with the necessary dispensation, made her definitive incorporation in Opus Dei on February 5, 1959. Normally this is only done when the member of the Work has reached at least five years past the age of consent and counts on years of fidelity to her vocation. Montse's situation was ample justification for an exception.

However, she was not keen on exceptions. "Do you think I deserve it?" she asked Lía. "You all consider me better than I am, but this time I don't care. I am so happy about it!"

"It was a very emotional occasion for her and for all of us," her mother recalls, "seeing her so happy and peaceful. Inés and Adela, my sisters, gave her a gold forget-me-not with her name and the date engraved on it; they brought her flowers, too, which that very night she sent to the tabernacle in Llar. We gave her a ring."

Choosing the ring – which symbolizes fidelity to our Lord's call – has a story of its own. Carmiña Cameselle takes up the story: "I knew a jeweller named Oriol; so I went to see him with Pilar Oriol, and her father-in-law lent us a showcase of rings to take with us."

"Montse chose one with such care!" recalls her mother; "she looked at one..., then another..., she chose one... she rejected it... As if she were going to wear it all her life...! With such joy!"

"In the end she decided on the simplest one of

all," Carmiña recalls, "but then, she asked her mother:

'Mom, which one do you like?'

'Now you choose the one you like best,' her mother who knew her well said, adding to encourage her: 'Look, when you have gone I will send the ring to the Father in Rome. So you had better choose the best one....'

'Then I'll take this one, Mom.'

"She chose a white gold one."

The juridical incorporation to Opus Dei was carried out in the normal way, very simply. There was a brief ceremony that finished with a prayer said by Don Florencio, Montse having read a longer one in front of a crucifix. In the prayer she had asked for *gaudium cum pace*, joy and peace, for everyone who persevered firmly in the service of God in Opus Dei.

"She was totally serene," reads the Llar diary, "once again giving us a lesson in generous and joyful self-giving. When everyone went out of the room there was a moment of such intense emotion that she could not hold back the tears; but they were tears of joy as well as fatigue due to the pain. She has been really ill these last few days."

All day long she kept looking at her ring. "I like looking at it," she said to Lía, "it reminds me to be faithful. It is very pretty, isn't it?"

Her father thought the occasion was worth a proper celebration. There was a bottle of champagne in the kitchen. He went to fetch it, drew the cork, and proposed a toast.

Montse raised her glass too, all smiles, perhaps recalling the toast of Christmas 1957 – so near and yet so far….

"The minute I arrived," Rosa recalls, "Montse blurted out: 'Rosa, I've made the commitment for life!'

"She was so excited, so full of joy, that I do not think her leg hurt that evening. She added:

'You can't imagine how lucky I am, Rosa! I have done it forever!' "

Squeezed like a lemon

Her visits to Llar were more spaced out now. Rosa recalls: "Every single journey was excruciating. One time, as we were coming down in the elevator from Llar, she threw her arms about my neck, in an agony of pain, saying: 'I can't stand it.' It is the only time I saw her with tears in her eyes."

She rarely cried. She was looking forward to going to heaven but, and there was a but, dying so young seemed to her too 'comfortable'. "But, I'm not doing anything!" she would say. She wanted to go on giving, suffering, loving. One day she said to the person taking care of her: "Do you realize that I am dying as the Father wishes those of Opus Dei to die: in a fine bed, surrounded by the loving care of everybody, but squeezed out like a lemon, with not a drop left."

The bit about the "fine bed" was only relative. It was a fine bed but not suitable for such a patient.

However it was difficult to find out if Montse was comfortable in it or not, as she never complained. Rosa had said to her ages ago: "Montse you would be much better off in one of those adjustable beds. You would be far more comfortable.... Shall I tell your parents to get you one?"

"Shush!" she always replied. "Don't you realize they have enough expenses already?"

Rosa says: "I am convinced that she was uncomfortable in that bed. When she did get a proper adjustable bed, which was much more comfortable, she recognized it was twice as good...." A friend of Manolita had lent them the bed.

Fidelity to God's grace was propelling Montse into a loving "crescendo" along the path of love, of total identification with Christ and his cross, to heights of contemplation that she could never have hoped for. Yes. It was the self-same Montse who just a couple of years previously had been bouncing on the beds for fun, to find the thickest and most comfortable mattress in Castelldaura before beginning her retreat....

Right now she was surrounded by everyone's loving care. In a thousand and one ways they tried to show it: by keeping quiet, by not putting the light on, by making her favorite meals...

It was difficult to avoid her having something she did not like as she ate everything. She accepted gracefully all the fuss they made of her. She happily ate whatever was there, recalling Encarnita's dictum: "Eat what's put in front of you."

However, one day "whatever was there" happened to be *elvers* (baby eels). Her aunt had brought her a good helping of these baby eels as a treat. This great delicacy was not normal fare for the Grases family and Montse wanted her aunt to see how grateful she was for her kindness.... However, having to eat elvers at that particular moment was real torture. One of the girls with her at the time said: "She began to eat and became very distressed. I tried to take the plate away several times. I was really sorry for her; she was exhausted and was trying so hard. She said she would eat it all, bit by bit, so as not to upset her aunt who had meant it as a treat."

The same kind of thing happened on other occasions when people tried to help. María del Carmen says: "Someone gave her a present of a small pillow to rest her head on. She tried it and said it bothered her a lot. But on reflection, to show appreciation to the person who had given her the pillow and had wanted to help her, she said she did not want it removed and she tried to convince us that it suited her."

❀   ❀   ❀

Her mother says: "Around February 11, the feast of Our Lady of Lourdes, she got worse; so we told all her friends not to come and visit her. She had no visitors for several days."

Those days were, externally, more peaceful. The hubbub of jokes and laughter that the Llar girls made when they came was absent. Life was becoming much more quiet on the outside; the incessant struggle to love God more continued on the inside.

"Some days later when we saw she was a bit better," her mother continues, "we let an occasional friend in to see her, although we did all we could not to overtire her.

"I went out to go to confession on one of those afternoons and when I got back the room was full of girls. I was afraid she would be exhausted, but I found her smiling and apparently enjoying herself, so I didn't worry. Her friends left early, since I had said they should not stay too long as it was the first day she was having visitors again.

"However, when she was alone again I realized she was quite exhausted and weary."

I won't be able to come again

"It was then that she left the house for the last time: it was actually February 15, 1959, a Sunday. In spite of her pitiful condition, they took her to Llar – not far by car – because they knew of her longing to celebrate the anniversary of the beginning of the women's section of Opus Dei" (which was on February 14, 1930).

Lía recalls that they celebrated the feast on the 15th because the day before was Saturday and the meditation given by the priest was at the same time. Montse went for lunch with the girls who lived in Llar. "She was exhausted when she arrived; it broke your heart to see her. Two of us helped her but she could hardly walk, it hurt her tremendously to be touched. She did not say anything but her face was expressive enough.

"She had a bad day. However, although she was suffering a lot she was talking, doing apostolate, and laughing with everyone, until we realized the effort she was having to make.... When we were left by ourselves she unburdened herself....

"After a while her mother called to ask her how she was and if she wanted her to come and fetch her. Montse said no, not to worry. I was surprised by her reply. But she pointed out: 'Do you know why? Mom is busy right now. It is dinnertime and then bedtime for the little ones and if she sees me like this she won't want to leave me alone.'

"Before leaving she went into the oratory to pray. She left, dragging her leg. It was heart-breaking.

"She took her leave of the director very simply with these words:

'Do you realize, Lía, that I won't be able to come again. I find walking more and more difficult. It's true that I won't be able to come, isn't it?' "

❀   ❀   ❀

"I remember when Montse Amat brought her in," her mother recalls. "She said: 'Manolita, she won't be able to go out again.'"

"Dr. Cañadell and his wife came that night, partly as doctor and partly as a friend. We wanted to celebrate the anniversary of the beginning of the apostolate with women of Opus Dei. Dr. Cañadell had operated on Jorge's knee and he was also in bed, nearly buried in comics. We went from one room to the other, Dr. Cañadell telling jokes all the while."

Jose Cañadell recalls: "My wife was in Montse's room. I could hear her singing and laughing. 'What are you celebrating?' Jorge inquired from his room. She shouted light-heartedly, referring to February 14 because besides being an anniversary it is also St. Valentine's day.

'Ah Jorge, haven't you heard that today is lover's day?'

"Now, with hindsight, Montse Amat's comment on the situation may seem melodramatic, but it did not appear so at the time: we carried on as if it were the most natural thing in the world, Montse in particular. There was no merit whatever on our part; it was Montse who made it all so easy...."

❀   ❀   ❀

"Montse made it all so easy." That is to say that she tried to head off all the sorrowful situations that often accompany a fatal illness. When the doctor came one morning, while he was taking her blood pressure, she inquired, "How am I?"

They all looked at each other. Dr. Cañadell paused briefly before saying, "You are on your way."

There was an embarrassing silence. No one knew what to say. More furtive glances... Montse solved the situation right then. She picked up a small black case – a useful item but not a particularly attractive design – which the doctor had left on the bed and said joking to her father.

"Look, Dad, what a pretty case...!"

❈   ❈   ❈

"A few days later, on February 22," her mother continues, "she inquired:

'Mom, aren't you praying a lot for me?'

'Of course I am, I replied. But what do you want me to pray for? For our Lord to help you to bear the suffering?'

"With a nod she agreed. Then I asked her:

'Aren't you sorry to be going?'

"She rose to the occasion with surprising energy, even though she was exhausted.

'No, not at all!'"

The root of all joy

Lía recalled how Montse "lived the Mass intensely, so much so that when she could no longer attend Mass because of her illness (a priest would take Communion to her every day) she offered up not being able to go as an act of penance. She just read the text of the Mass of the day and joined in with the intentions of the priest."

Dr. Cañadell recalls a daily happening. It reveals where the root of Montse's cheerfulness can be found. "She received Holy Communion every day and she often went to confession. I know this to be the case as my visit often coincided with the priest's, and I would have to wait until she had finished her thanksgiving after Communion."

Tiredness and sleepless nights sometimes would make Montse fall asleep during her thanksgiving. She always asked us to keep her awake. She maintained that Communion gave her the strength to continue her struggle: without the Eucharist she could not live.

The Eucharist and confession, "the Sacrament of Joy", were the fundamental keys to understanding the strength behind Montse's smile. She found the strength, grace, and the whole point of enduring pain in these sacraments and in her life of piety. She would ask herself, "What would become of me without the Eucharist? What would I have done if I had not been able to receive our Lord daily?"

Pilar Martin writes: "You just had to see her

practice her norms of piety to know where her strength came from."

The priest who took Communion to Montse noticed how she often repeated: "May the holy will of God be done," as well as other aspirations that echo the unmistakable words of the founder of Opus Dei. For instance: "May the most just and most lovable will of God be done, be fulfilled, be praised and eternally exalted above all things. Amen. Amen."

❦   ❦   ❦

"I used to look at her," her father continues, "and I was mesmerized..., as if that daughter of mine had suddenly matured humanly and spiritually.... She was travelling the long road to possession of God in leaps and bounds, almost without realizing it, during the last months of her illness.... Normally it takes people a lifetime.

"I stood by amazed to see how, day by day, she was nearing the death I had always wanted for myself: in God's presence, with the abandonment proper to the spirit of Opus Dei, with apostolic zeal and selflessness that inspired her to think only of others, not complaining during those awful dressings, being aware of her mother's need to rest... and all the time full of incredible good cheer, which did not allow any of us to be sad....

She even went to the extreme of doing what

was physically for her the most daunting thing of all: to dance. She did this so that we would be cheered. I shall never forget one particular morning. As the dressings were normally changed early in the morning, I would return from the office for a while because at least three people were needed to help with the dressings. She did not want me to have to leave my work to come and care for her, so she scolded me gently. One day I was helping her to stand in the corridor while they were making the bed. She was already very ill, quite weak.... She must have seen my sorrow. I don't really know. But the fact is, that to lighten my suffering, she said, 'Dad, come on, let's dance...' and she took my arm and we tried to dance for a few moments...."

❦   ❦   ❦

That same day, February 23, Lía, who had been away for a few days, went to see her.

"The first thing I did when I got back was to go and see Montse," she recalls; "and I was horrified. She was like death. She hardly opened her eyes when I came in. Her mother was there and made signs to me to sit down and be quiet.

"She had had a couple of really bad days, and they thought they would have to call me....

"She was very worried as in this situation she could not do her norms of piety well.... I reassured her, saying that her prayer now consisted in giving her suffering generously to our Lord.

"She said she was already doing that.

'At nighttime, when I can't sleep, I think of each one of you....'"

Exhaustion and pain were taking their toll. As Fr. Manuel Vall pointed out, she struggled heroically to fulfill her norms of piety, in spite of it being so difficult in her circumstances; physically she was hardly able to do them at all. She asked for some of her friends to come and help her to pray, especially the ones she had been praying for to God for a vocation. She wanted to do everything in her power to spur them on in their commitment to God.

Although she was exhausted she took care of the small details in her life of piety. She really tried to say the rosary well, as well as everything referring to our Lady. Lía recalls: "Her devotion to our Lady was like the background music to her life of piety." Although her strength was ebbing, she took exquisite care of the prayer, making notes in her diary of her resolutions after her examination of conscience. On the 23rd, Monday night, she wrote: "Prayer: better, more inclination. Communion: it was hard work but I made an effort. Holy Rosary: one part, good, not so the other two..."

She did her examination of conscience thoroughly; in a small, simple, blue notebook she would write down her resolutions every night. It was not really a diary; she never kept one.

María Teresa Gonzalez was another person

who used to come and sit with Montse, and she tells how "one night she started to do her examination of conscience as usual. She was at the stage when she spent long periods of the day in a semi-conscious state. Her mother and I were present. She realized she had not done all her norms of piety. She was almost in tears when she said she had only prayed two parts of the rosary and had not made the visit to the Blessed Sacrament at all. We calmed her down and said we would do it now, but she said plaintively:

'Do you know what, I just can't.'

'Do you want to say it?' I inquired.

'Of course I want to!'

'Then don't worry, we will do the praying, you just listen.'

"And she settled down. We just said the three Our Fathers of the visit to the Blessed Sacrament. She followed the prayers with great fervor although you could hardly hear her."

When she was praying

Rosa says: "I was profoundly impressed when she prayed. When she was praying it was like... look, I don't know how the saints pray, but for me it was like watching a saint pray. Sometimes, in the middle of an acute attack of severe pain, she would suddenly say, 'Rosa, let's do the prayer.' During the half an hour the prayer lasted I would read from some spiritual book, while she was like... I can't explain it... I had the feeling she was very, very close to our Lord. It really got to me…."

"I could not understand how she could be so quiet and so devout in the midst of such pain…. Like this, a bit more every day. I saw her become more united with our Lord, minute by minute, over the period of her illness. It was such a rapid profound change that one day I asked her:

'Montse, you are the same Montse as always, aren't you?'

"She said she was; but she felt the proximity of heaven, which spurred her on in her struggle.

"I was amazed how she had identified herself completely with the will of God. She often explained how everything God sends us we should accept as coming from his hand. She let herself be taken by his hand. She was teaching me with her own life what our founder said: having the cross means finding happiness and joy; it is identifying oneself with Christ, being Christ and therefore a child of God. 'What can a child fear if he knows his father is God?'

"She was very grateful. The day I bade farewell she thanked me for everything; she assured me she would pray specially for me in heaven, so that I would continue to be happy. She said so many wonderful things to me that I shall never forget them.

"At the end, the last two weeks of her life, they said she was quite exhausted and it was better for me not to go to see her. They wanted her to rest those last painful days..."

They had to reduce the number of visitors as she had had continual visits from her friends. Her mother recalls: "When we heard the elevator coming up we would catch our breath and relax again when our doorbell did not ring. There was a doctor living on the same floor as us. He held a surgery in his home three days a week. When we heard steps we would say: 'Dr. Saenz has patients today.'

"But we were often wrong and the room was filled with friends. Montse always received them with a smile even though she was exhausted; though she found it hard to speak, she would always try to say something to bring them nearer to God. But at the end, when they were going, she would slump, overwhelmed, and say:

'I couldn't go on, Mom.'

"I would try to screen some of them. But she would never say no.... One day two friends came and said to me:

'Don't tell her we are here. Just say we have called on the phone to see if we can come. I thought it was better to tell her clearly. 'Montse, two girls have come and they want to see you. They think you are not aware of them being here; so tell me frankly, Montsina, do you feel like having them come in for a little while? If you don't, you don't have to....'

'Mom,' she replied, 'we are not here to do what we feel like. Show them in.'"

Although her life was fading away, these visits took place in a peaceful, happy atmosphere.

Montse Amat recalls: "Everybody who went to see her during her illness came out deeply impressed. One of her friends said: 'Whenever I went I always came out with a sense of peace, wanting to be a better person. I never came out sad.'" One of her mother's friends, Montserrat Raventós, put it succinctly: "A visit to Montse really pays off !"

She would often begin to pray, and promptly fall asleep, overcome by the pain. Suddenly she would wake up for a little while and say to whoever was with her. "Why didn't you wake me? Can't you see I haven't finished the prayer yet?" To put her mind at rest they would tell her not to worry, to offer up this problem, and that in itself would be prayer. She would answer...

"Well, I am doing the prayer all day in that case, because I offer up everything. What I want to do is carry out my plan of life."

She said to Lía: "The prayer is really hard for me. I cannot coordinate ideas; I would like to, it is just that I am a bit stupid...."

"Don't worry Montse. Offering up your suffering wholeheartedly is precisely the most pleasing prayer to God. Remember that point in *The Way*: 'An hour of study, for a modern apostle, is an hour of prayer.' The Father would surely say to you that an hour of suffering is an hour of prayer."

"Yes. That is true," she would agree, in a slightly sad tone of voice. "It is the only thing I have to offer...."

"But Montse, don't you believe in the value of

suffering?"

"Yes, but it is so little.... However our lives are like that: we must keep giving of ourselves, as the Father says, squeezed out like a lemon...."

Montse Amat tells: "I spent a lot of time with her in those last days, as Lía and I took turns spending the night with her." She was impressed by Montse's lively interest in doing the pious practices of her Christian plan of life. "When you did not know what to do for her, she would ask peacefully:

'Shall we do one of our norms?'

She was concerned about whoever stayed the night with her. One of them says, "She would always ask if we were cold, if we would like a drink.... Sometimes I would hear her whisper.

'Do you want something Montse?' I would ask.

'No,' she would reply. 'I am just saying aspirations....'"

Montse Amat also recalls how one of those days they began to say the rosary. "Seeing how ill she was, I asked her if she had the strength to say it. She replied:

'Yes, I do want to say it.' Montse prayed in silence and every time she finished a Hail Mary, she made a sign so I could go on."

It became more difficult for her to sustain a conversation for any length of time; but if her ring had to come off for whatever reason, she would put out her hand for it to be put back on again. (The ring reminded her to be faithful to God in Opus Dei.)

Also if she lost her crucifix, a present from the Father, among the bed sheets, she would look for it until she found it and then kiss it lovingly. Sometimes, she would adjust the bed-sheets with just two fingers – a typical gesture of hers – because she insisted on holding the crucifix in her hand.... "I like to have it near," she told Lía. "I need it most during the night."

One of the girls relates: "One night, after doing the examination of conscience, she stretched out her hand as if looking for something. I asked her what she wanted. She indicated that we had forgotten to use holy water. She had the habit of sprinkling the bed with holy water, calling on God to protect her throughout the night." It is one of those age-old Christian devotions that members of Opus Dei practice. It is recommended by many saints, among them St. Teresa of Avila who said: "There is nothing like holy water to frighten devils and keep them away."

In spite of her exhaustion, Montse was solicitous towards others. She was concerned for her mother's rest. One night as soon as Lía arrived she said:

"Lía, let us try to get Mom to bed. She always wants to stay up the first part of the night , as I give most trouble then and I'd rather she didn't. Don't you think it's a good idea to play a little trick? When Mom comes and says she wants to stay up till five, what do you think if I say 'we'll draw lots'? Look, you point to this hand. Later on I will tell you which medicine you have to give me, so she can get some sleep."

A farewell hug

Her mother recalls: "On the morning of March 8, I told Montse: 'If you agree, we have been thinking that perhaps this afternoon you should receive Extreme Unction.... You know it is a sacrament of the living, don't you? And, right now, you are in full possession of your faculties.... Besides, this sacrament is to ask for health if it is appropriate, among many other benefits....'

'Whatever you like,' she replied at once. Lía and I were at her side. She became quiet for a few moments, and then asked Lía:

'Lía, how do I look to you?'

'You look very ill,' Lía answered. 'How do you feel?'

'Actually I feel very weak, exhausted, tired out....'

"Then she made a bemused smiling gesture. Lía was surprised to see the change.

'No,' she said smiling. 'I am not laughing at you, Lía; I am just amused by the face you make.'

She was silent for a while. Then referring to death she said:

'What will happen, Mom? How will it happen?'

'Montse, I think you will go from sleep straight to heaven.'

"I said so quite convinced that it could very well be like that, because often I would be sitting by her side as she lay half-asleep, I would take her hand

and feel for her pulse….

'How very comfortable! No suffering!' she said with a worried look.

'Comfortable?' I said to her astounded. And I began to enumerate all the discomforts of her suffering: changing the dressings, the thirst, lack of appetite, not being able to move...

'Indeed, all of that's true; but it is so little.... Won't they have to operate on me or some such thing? Like this, it is quite easy to do….'

"Then she smiled again, became silent, and later said:

'Well, if it is like that, we are not going to be able to say farewell.'

'Shall we do it now?' I asked.

'Yes, let's.'

"Then I knelt down beside her bed and we had a big long hug….

"After that farewell hug," her mother continues, "she began to deteriorate, so much so that she had difficulty in breathing.... I was very worried, thinking that maybe she would die of asphyxiation. I was afraid she would think her mother had betrayed her at the last moment…. Dr. Cañadell had warned me that death could come in one of these turns."

Extreme Unction

"That night her father explained the sacrament of Anointing of the Sick, then called Extreme Unction, in great detail, so she could take full advantage of it," Carmiña recalls.

"He said: 'Look darling, when the priest comes, first of all he will make the sign of the cross on your forehead with oil. At that moment try to ask for forgiveness for all thoughts, faults against charity, or rash judgments that could have separated you from our Lord...'

"Her mother and I were also in the room in total silence. He went on:

'Then the priest will make the sign of the cross on your chest, above your heart. You should ask our Lord for pardon for the less virtuous intentions and feelings.'"

Don Florencio came in the afternoon and administered Extreme Unction, first explaining each liturgical act. Her parents and the older children were there, as well as Lía, Carmiña, María Teresa... Her mother kept smiling all the time to keep her going.

Later on when Don Florencio had gone, Montse asked:

"When is it all going to end? I am really looking forward to going...."

They told her that maybe our Lord wished her to continue helping many souls, the Church, the Father, and Opus Dei by offering up her sufferings to God.

"Then I don't mind a few more days. Or whenever our Lord wills."

❀   ❀   ❀

Carmiña recalls: "Some of her brothers and sisters were present while she was receiving Extreme Unction: Enrique, who was home from the seminary, Jorge, Pilar, and Nacho, who was thirteen at the time. The twins were not there, nor was Rafael, the little one. When it was over, Nacho came out with his eyes full of tears. Then Enrique came out. He was crying too and they stayed together. Enrique said: 'Nacho, don't cry. Montse is dying very happily, because she is going to heaven and won't have to suffer any more....'

"Those of us who witnessed the scene were very moved. Just then Montse's father said jokingly to break the tension:

'You see, Enrique is preparing to be a priest.... He is already preaching sermons to his brother....'

"We all laughed."

Yes, I can

The 8th of March was a strenuous day. Montse Amat narrates how "that night Montse was worn out; she could not even write her examination of conscience in her notebook. I told her not to worry, just to do it without writing anything down.

"She began and after a little while making a big effort, she said:

'Give me the notebook, yes I can do it.' And she did it just like any other night."

The last days of her illness dragged on, hard

and relentless. The Eucharist sustained her, she received our Lord every day. As she found it very hard to swallow, she had to help herself with a sip of water.

One day two friends came to see her; on leaving, they said they were going to Llar where they would have Benediction. "How I envy you!" she exclaimed. When she was doing the prayer she could not avoid uttering a plea aloud, directed to the image of our Lady, in her room.

"Mother, when will you take me?"

However, she did not let impatience take over, even though sometimes pain got the upper hand. Montse Amat recalls: "One night, Lía and I were with her, when a kind of sigh escaped her.

'I cannot go on any longer....'

"We helped her to change her position and fluffed up her pillow to make her feel more comfortable. Then she added offering up her pain: 'Yes I can. I can, for the Father, of course....'"

❀   ❀   ❀

The notes she made after her examination of conscience those last days bear witness to her daily struggle to live devoutly the customs of Christian piety, proper to a person of Opus Dei, even though she was physically exhausted. Her daily examination of conscience was not that of a perfectionist or a scrupulous search for her own faults. Rather, as the founder taught, "it was prompted by love." At the end of the examination, she made an act of contrition and petition for grace for the next day .

On Sunday, the 8th, she wrote: "The prayer late and half asleep, but I tried." The 9th: "Prayer, OK. Communion, better." The 10th: "Afternoon prayer, OK; Communion, OK; two parts of the rosary, OK. Communion, OK... Particular exam, much better. Some moments of despondency. Later on, cheerful."

Right up to the end she had to struggle against her hot temper. On Friday the 13th she noted "Afternoon prayer, OK; irritable."

On the 14th: "Anxiety and lack of peace. Later on, fine." On the 15th she made her last annotation. "Lack of peace and anxiety, kind of lonely."

The sensation of loneliness – together with doubts, fears, and temptation that our Lord permits many souls to suffer so as to purify them – was possibly one of the last trials Montse had to endure in this world.

❀   ❀   ❀

"One day when I arrived I noticed she was very agitated," Carmiña relates. "Even though I did not know what the matter was, I remember that the dying frequently suffer many temptations during the last days, especially against the virtue of hope.... So I said:

'Look Montse, when the devil sees a person on the point of death, he fights the last battle; because the devil does exist and he tempts us and doesn't leave us alone until the last minute. Right now maybe you have many temptations against hope. Don't worry; call on our Lady. Trust her. Don't be frightened by what is happening to you. It is not your fault. Imagine for instance there is a fly on the window pane. We have not put it there, we cannot get rid of it; but we don't have to take any notice of it, counting its wings or looking what color it is.... A doubt, about whether you are going to be condemned or not, can assail you; or you can have a temptation against hope: or maybe you can even think: How unjust God is to take my life in the flower of youth.... Don't worry: just pray, trust our Lady, and call on her.'

"She agreed. After a little while she said:

'Eh, Carmiña: What color are our Lady's eyes? Blue or green?'

'I don't know,' I replied, surprised. 'Maybe they are green....'

"And looking at Our Lady of Montserrat, she exclaimed:

'My mother, I love you. I love you! My mother, I love you!'...."

St. Joseph's day

"The night of the 16th to the 17th we thought she was dying, and we called the doctor at four o'clock in the morning because she was really bad," her mother says. "She was very happy because she thought the moment had come…. The doctor came at six in the morning and said he found her worse. Her pulse was strong but her breathing was very labored and she was very thirsty: She could hardly drink and she even choked on just a sip of water."

"Then the doctor said, 'I don't think she will last past tomorrow,'" Carmiña recalls.

"Do you know something, Montse," her father said, "the doctor says that maybe you will go tomorrow."

"Really, Mom," she exclaimed happily. "I am going to go now. Jorge, do you realize? Heaven forever. Do you realize, Jorge? I am going to heaven. To heaven!"

"Yes, darling," her father said sorrowfully. "You are going and you will be very happy... But we are going to miss you…. When Rafita grows up…. When Enrique is ordained…."

"But Dad... I am going to see everything from heaven! I am going to pray for all of you from there." And she went on telling her father all the things she would do for them in heaven.

"The news of her imminent death had lit up her face with a smile of happiness. Heaven was already very near! She began to ask St. Joseph to come and fetch her, and to say, 'Jesus, Mary, and Joseph, may I breathe forth my soul in peace with you.'"

What will heaven be like?

"Tell me what heaven will be like," she inquired.

"Something fabulous that I can't describe, but I am certain that you are going to be very happy...." Lía said.

"Imagine, heaven forever," she exclaimed. "It is too much, Lord. I don't deserve it."

Then she turned to Lía and said, very earnestly: "You have to help me a lot. Do you know, I am afraid?"

And then suddenly, making a gesture with her hand as if including everything, she said:

"Everybody. I want everybody to pray for me. I love you all very, very much...."

Silence fell. Then she asked Lía again:

"Lía, do you think our Lord wants me in heaven? Sometimes I have a really bad time. It is like temptations, which come and go.... But if you say that I will go to heaven, I do believe you...."

"It is so wonderful that I can't explain it," Lía continued. "But of this much I am certain, you are going to be very happy.... Do you remember reading St. Teresa, where she says she feels incapable of telling, because words are not adequate to express how it is? Well, how do you expect me to explain it to you, when I haven't seen it?"

"Then she grabbed my hand," Lía says, "and said:

'Tell me, say it over and over again... I will go to heaven....'

"So I did, several times, and then she exclaimed in a loud voice:

'But when, My Lord?'

"She added almost shouting:

'Mary, my Mother. I love you so very much!' Then she lowered her voice and said:

'I am silly, really; but if I don't shout it, it seems to me as if I didn't say it at all....'

"She closed her eyes and began to say aspirations: 'Jesus, Jesus, Jesus...' and then she fell asleep."

❀   ❀   ❀

"María Campí came very early on the morning of the 18th so we could go to Mass," Lía continues. "Montse Amat left for Mass with Montse's parents. I wanted to go, too, but Montse didn't want me to leave her, so I stayed. She held my hand firmly.

'Lía, what will heaven be like?' she asked me again.

"I told her as best I could; that it was a wonderful place, very near God....

'Do you realize that you are going to see the Grandmother and Aunt Carmen and all the people of Opus Dei who have already died? Can you imagine what a welcome they are going to give you? What joy there will be in heaven...! Don't forget to tell God lots of things about us and to pray for the Father's intentions.... Isidoro will be there too; he will be delighted to see you, what with all the interceding we have directed his way...!'"

Lía concludes: "...She was silent for a while. Then suddenly she began to clap and said:

'Wonderful! Tomorrow is St. Joseph's feast day. He will come to fetch me, so I am off to heaven!'"

❀   ❀   ❀

The feast day of St. Joseph dawned. She dreamt this was her day, her *dies natalis*, her birthday in heaven. As the founder of Opus Dei had taught us, it was the day when we would meet, at last!, with Love himself, with all the beauty, grandeur, richness, harmony and color that Love entails.... She had spent the previous evening saying aspirations:

"St. Joseph's Day is tomorrow; I am off tomorrow. The patron of a happy death is coming to get me.... Jesus, Mary, and Joseph, assist me now and in my last agony.... Jesus, Mary, and Joseph, may I breathe forth my soul in peace with you."

Fr. Emilio Navarro went to see her. He recalls that "she inquired about the girls who go to Llar. She told me she was pleased because thanks to her illness some friends of hers had become involved with Opus Dei.... I found her peaceful, tired, yes, but without any worries of any kind. I remember we talked about Bartolo Llorens, a member of Opus Dei who had died a few years previously soon after requesting the admission, just like herself, and how he had offered up all his sufferings for the apostolates of the Work....."

The hours of the feast day of the Holy Patriarch were slipping by... to no avail! And the irony of it was she even felt a little better that afternoon....

Lía recalls: "She said nothing about it, not even a hint." At midnight the two of them prayed for the intentions of the founder: "*Misericordia Domini ab aeterno et usque in aeternum super eum: custodit enim Dominus omnes diligentes se...*"

Lía concludes: "And then she said, sorrowfully,:

'Do you know what? I think I feel a bit better...'"

❀   ❀   ❀

Our Lord asked the sacrifice of this last wish of hers – to die on St. Joseph's day.

"She was in a pre-agony state from a medical viewpoint, with great breathing difficulties,"

Fr. Emilio Navarro recalls. He went to see her the following afternoon. "They had to help her to sit up a bit so that she could get her breath. She was in great pain and disappointed that she had not died the previous day. And one had to try to console her in some way or other.... I said: 'Look Montse, if God leaves you here with us, it must be for a reason. Maybe our Lord wants you to come to him more purified and to continue offering up your suffering to him....'"

"She accepted that. Shortly afterwards she said to Lía: "Do you know what I think? I am not going to worry any longer. Whenever God wills he'll take me."

Her parents did not lose hope... and just like all other days, they prayed the novena to Isidoro. However, on this occasion, towards the end of the prayer... *and to be an apostle of my friends and companions: deign to glorify your servant and through his intercession grant me the favor I ask of you,* he said the petition, which everyone had already said in their hearts, aloud: "for Montse's health."

"I was kneeling by Montse's bed," Lía tells, "and she took my hand and said:

'You wouldn't pray for that, would you?'

'What do you want me to pray for?'

'For me to go to heaven soon.'"

Soon afterwards Manuel Grases said good-bye

to his daughter, as he did every day on his way to work. Montse inquired:

"Dad, will you let me go?"

"Go where, Montse?" Not understanding her question, he asked: "Where do you want to go to?"

"Dad, for goodness sake!" she replied firmly. "Heaven. I want to go to heaven!"

❀   ❀   ❀

The hours of March 20 passed with progressive breathing problems. She felt very tired and overwhelmed.

Dr. Cañadell came to confirm that her deterioration had reached alarming extremes, complicated by pulmonary metastasis. This is what caused the breathing difficulties. She was observing the doctor. Suddenly she said to him, "Is there much longer to go?"

"Montse, that depends on God," José Cañadell replied. "However, from a medical viewpoint, you can consider that there is still quite some way to go."

"On leaving the house," Manuel Grases says, "the doctor, out of earshot, said it could be a question of hours or a few days at most. When we returned to her side, Montse said:

'You see Dad, St. Joseph did not take me.... I am so tired! When will it be?'

"I knew Montse had such longing to be with

our Lord and I wanted so much to see her happy after such a lot of suffering that to console her, I was inexplicably moved to say:

'Look Montse, without doubt only God knows the day and the hour. But you can be sure that you will be by his side in heaven on Easter Sunday.'

"Montse put her arms around me while she exclaimed.

'Oh no, Dad! Not so far away! I want it with all my might! Is there long to go?'

'No, Montse. Only nine days.'

"Then she smiled happily and lay back to rest."

The solemn celebrations of Holy Week were imminent. A Holy Week in which our Lord made her participate intimately with the sufferings of his Passion. She lived those days closely united to the cross, physically too: in the midst of all her suffering she never abandoned the crucifix the Father had given her. She kept it in her hands all the time. She wore the ring all the time too.

Carmiña relates: "As she was so weak, she dropped the crucifix quite often, so she asked us to put it around her neck. Then she would caress it with her fingers and thus unite her ring with the cross. That is how she spent those awful nights."

She would try to speak but they could hardly understand her. She kept on thinking about heaven.

"I am so selfish," she said to Lía, "I keep on thinking about heaven...."

"You do well, Montse. It is only just that you

should start enjoying it and thinking about the reward. Anyway you are still here and we need you to pray for us."

"I will do it there too, don't you worry."

Some girls, who had recently requested admission to Opus Dei, came to see her. Among other words of greeting, she said to them:

"Be faithful. It is worthwhile. Be faithful."

❀   ❀   ❀

She became weaker. They called the doctor who came and examined her. He went out of the room to speak to her parents. They all came back except for the doctor.

"What did the doctor say?" she inquired of one of those present, who, in turn, looked at Manolita not knowing what to say.

"Tell her," she said, "don't you see with what a smiling face she asks?"

"Well, Montse, he says you can go at any moment."

"Then she gave her a big hug," her mother says, "as if she had just given her really good news."

Her desire "to go" was the result of love. A love "stronger than death," as we read in scripture; however, this love did not take away the very human fear, when confronting such a definitive step, expressed in the poem she had transcribed so long ago:

Do not leave me Jesus, night falls and
faith is waning!
>*The shadows lengthen, my God*
>*And the world cannot see!*
>*Stay with me please, don't leave me*
>*Because You are my Love!*
>*A cloud pours out*
>*Its burden of sorrow in my mind!*

❀   ❀   ❀

"It was on one of those nights," her mother recalls, "that she said with a look reflecting her anxiety.

'Mom, I am afraid....'

"It was as if she felt guilty of being afraid. I said:

'Montse, it is normal for you to be afraid... that is not wrong. Don't you remember Jesus in the Garden of Gethsemani, how he was afraid and asked God: "Father, if it is possible let this chalice pass from me?"'

"I tried to pacify her in my way, but she still thought she was lacking in something...."

The hours dragged by that day. Montse impatiently awaited Lía's arrival in the early afternoon.

"You have taken so long about coming today, Lía," she said to her on arrival.

"But, Montse, I have come at the same time as always...."

"I know," she said, her voice hesitant and weary, "but I was anxious to see you because I have lots to tell you. Do you know I am afraid of death again. I have been really frightened: I have been doubting the existence of heaven, maybe it is all a sham...."

"But Montse, can you doubt for a second that we, your father, your mother, all of us here with you, love you?"

"No, I don't," she said with determination.

"Well, then how can you doubt our Lord, who loves you to the extreme of giving you the strength to stand all this. Even though you say it is not so bad, I know it is...."

"Yes, indeed. Everything you say is true, but I am afraid of not being brave enough, and I am terrified of death and suffering...."

"Our Lord was afraid too, in the Garden of Olives. You remember he exclaimed: 'Father, let this chalice pass from me... but thy will be done....' Why should you not be afraid too?"

"I don't want to be afraid but," touching her temple, "I have such strange thoughts and I wish I hadn't... Why don't you sprinkle some holy water on my pillow? I have been thinking about the coffin too and it frightens me...."

"Why do you think about things like that? Look here, your soul is worth far more than your body and we will treat your body really well, because we love you so much. Try not to think about it. Just think about your soul which is so beautiful. God is waiting for it to fill it with happiness..."

"True. How silly of me. Lía, promise me you won't leave me until the very end?"

"I promise you, Montse. I will be here with you, right up to the last second, until you leave us."

"And I promise you that I won't forsake you. I will help you a lot from above...."

"She was quite exhausted by the conversation. I encouraged her to relax a while and she did. Now and again she moved her lips in a quiet murmur. I asked her: 'Are you trying to say something to me.' 'No, I am just saying aspirations.' "

❀   ❀   ❀

"I was very glad," her mother relates, "that Fr. Emilio Navarro came to see her that same evening. As soon as he arrived I told him of our conversation the day before. He entered the room. Montse was very tired, and Fr. Emilio told her not to worry if she could not reply.

'Can you hear me, Montse? I want you to remember the agony of our Lord Jesus Christ in the Garden of Gethsemani shortly before his Passion. We read in the Gospels how Jesus was afraid...'

"I was amazed how the three of us, Fr. Emilio, Lía, and I, had all said the same thing.... She became very peaceful. I never saw her worried again. She was even happier than before. One day, we were both quietly alone when she suddenly looked at me and said:

'Mom, how very happy we are!'"

Palm Sunday

That particular Palm Sunday was very different! There was none of the noisy excitement of previous years when all the children set out with their palms, and their father would get out his movie camera to film the little ones hanging onto their palms for all they were worth, as they waved to and fro in the breeze. Now it was silence surrounding Montse. The palm Rosa sent her was placed beside the image of our Lady.

Lía spent the whole evening by her side. Montse was very lethargic. Now and again she would wake up and talk a bit. "At one particular moment," Lía recalls, "she sat straight up and began to shout aspirations. She kissed the crucifix frequently and said very quietly, although she could hardly speak:

'Lord, I love you very, very much and our Lady too.'

"I tried to calm her down.

'Montse, relax, quiet, calm down. Our Lord knows you love him very much...! Tell him quietly. I will go on saying aspirations and you can repeat them.'

'Yes, Lía. But do you know what the trouble is? I think that if I don't say them like that, he won't hear me. And I do want to say that I love him very very much, often...!'"

Lía began to say some of the aspirations the founder of Opus Dei taught her.

"Sweet Heart of Mary, prepare a safe way for us... Sacred Heart of Jesus, give us peace... Jesus, Jesus may you always be Jesus for me...."

"However the aspiration I heard her say most often," her mother recalls, "was: 'Whenever you like, wherever you like, as you like....'"

❀   ❀   ❀

One day they were talking again about our Lady.

"I will see her soon, won't I?" asked Montse, with a big smile.

"I am sure you will, as soon as you arrive," Lía told her.

"I love her too, such a lot."

Her impetuous desire to be with God did not separate her from those around her. Lía advised her not to have her friends visit because she was exhausted by the length of time (two or three hours) it took to do the dressings; even though they did their utmost, it was extremely painful. Sometimes

they would have to take a break, as she was passing
out. But Montse thought it was what she had to offer
to God at that moment....

She carried on with her efforts to love God
more, although now she could not even read. "Read
something about love for me from *The Way*," she
asked on one occasion. Some time previously she
had written this prayer to our Lady in her note book:
"My mother, for all my infidelities, tell our Lord
never again. My mother, for all the silly things I do
every day, tell our Lord never again. My mother, but
you know I will fall again."

She kept uniting herself to Jesus' total self-
giving on Calvary. "Help me to be brave," she
asked, "I need it so much."

"Montse," Lía said devotedly, "don't say that
again, because if you do I will get cross. You know
you are brave."

"Do you really think I am?"

"When I said she was, that she was putting up
with so much," Lía recalls, "she gave me a hug and
said, 'It gives me great peace to hear you say so.'"

Monday of Holy Week

Lía was at Montse's bedside all of Palm
Sunday night. Next day, Monday of Holy Week, Lía
wrote to Encarnita Ortega in Rome:

"She was saying to me last night: 'Lía, how
slow it is. I never knew it was so difficult to die. But
do you know what? I am really happy. It seems that

he still needs me.' She made a very meaningful gesture while she clenched her fist, squeezed out like a lemon. She never tires of repeating over and over again: 'I want you all to know that I am very happy.' You can't imagine how impressive it is to hear her. She has great difficulty now in speaking... because she is almost gone. But it is amazing how cheerful she is, her face lights up when we tell her she will be going to heaven soon, she is so anxious to be there!"

Tuesday of Holy Week

On the 24th, Tuesday of Holy Week, Montse was so tired that they decided not to change her dressings at all. Perhaps she would be a little better the next day....

Soon afterwards Dr. Cañadell came. He had a look at Montse and then spoke to Manuel and Manolita in another room, not leaving until a quarter to eight. When Lía came back into her room Montse asked:

"What did the doctor say?"

"There is no change."

"Yes, but I feel something inside that tells me that I am going ahead and every day I get through...." She turned to her mother.

"Mom, thank you for helping me so much, you and Dad and Lía... all the time. Mom, you have always been there...! You have meant so much to me!... So very much in my life!"

Among those who often came to visit her was

María Luisa Xiol's mother. She would inquire every day how Montse was. Relatives, friends, and neighbors called constantly.... But her parents had decided she would not see anyone, as she was completely exhausted.

No one should see her. But even so, how could they not make an exception for Rosa?

Rosa says: "Her mother telephoned my home to tell me to come immediately, because Montse was dying.... At that moment I was out, and my mother said, 'I don't know where exactly Rosa is. But I know she has gone out for tea with some friends.'

"She then called Lezo's. She knew that I often went to this particular restaurant to have tea with Montse. Ever since she became ill I always left her the phone number of where we were going, so she would not worry. She found me there.

"I went to Montse's at once. It was Tuesday of Holy Week. Mrs. Grases warned me: 'Rosa, you will be shocked to see her, she is so changed... Our Lord is going to take her and we have to accept his will. She was delighted to get your palm on Palm Sunday and asked us to put it next to our Lady at once....' I was trembling.... Quite a few days, maybe three weeks, had passed since I had seen her. I was truly shocked to see her like that. She was... a living skeleton. The poor darling was a complete wreck. You could see her teeth through the skin of her cheeks. She was skin and bones.

They woke her up. 'Look, Montse. Look, Rosa has come to say good-bye to you.' She looked at me and recognized me. But she could not say anything. She moved her gaze to the palm I had sent her a few days previously, and squeezed my hand. I gave her a kiss and I whispered into her ear for her to remember me. She smiled and with her head and her eyes she acknowledged she would…. Her mother told me she was going to receive Holy Communion. But I was overcome. I felt unable to cope, so I left."

Spy Wednesday

March 25 dawned, the day the Church celebrates the Annunciation. That year the feast was eclipsed by the celebration of Wednesday in Holy Week, which presages the imminent Passion of our Lord. Her mother realized the end was near. Montse could hardly speak. Manuel, the older children, Lía, Montse Amat, and a few others stayed by her bed, day and night. She was in a state of semi-coma most of the time. At a given moment she opened her eyes, and making a great effort to pronounce the words she said, "How much I love you!"

Later on she added: "I love you all very much. But I love our Lord much more."

❀   ❀   ❀

That same afternoon Fr. Emilio Navarro went to visit her. Montse was rapidly getting worse: a few times she had tried to speak but she could not. Fr. Emilio tried to understand what she was trying to say; he called her mother, who could not understand either. Then, by signs, Montse asked for a pencil and paper. Pulling on all her strength she weakly traced the name of her seminarian brother. They came to the conclusion she was asking Fr. Emilio to take care of his priestly vocation.

Go to Llar

They had not changed her dressing for two days, because of the state she was in. At a particular moment her parents observed she was a little better. There was no time to lose: they decided to take advantage of this moment of relative improvement to change the dressing.

It was a long, painful process, longer and more painful than usual. When they got the bandage off they found her leg soaked in blood. Frightened they called the doctor. He reassured them. It was only caused by the rupture of a small vein.

During the process, at the precise moment of discovering the burst vein in her knee, there was a knock at the door. It was Mrs. Xiol with her two daughters, Ana and María Luisa, who had come down to see her from Llerona, where they were spending Holy Week. They asked them to wait in the sitting room. Meantime, in Montse's room, those looking after her were still worried about her hemorhagc, although it soon stopped. They carried on with the long tedious process. They removed the bandages, trying to avoid any movement that could hurt her.

Time passed with Mrs. Xiol and her daughters still waiting in the sitting room. It was late and Manolita thought it best for them to wait until Montse was asleep or if they did not mind, they could come back another time. Anyway she went in to tell Montse.

"Montse, María Luisa, Ana María, and their mother arc out there. They have come to see you. I have told them how you are and that it is better they don't come in. Don't you worry. I will spend a while with them and when you are asleep they can come in for a second…."

"No," she said in the weakest whisper. "I want to see them." "They entered the room. She indicated to them by a sign that she could not speak. She tried to say something, but they did not understand.

"Then," her mother recalls, "she asked me to come close and she whispered into my ear:

'Mom, tell her that my last will is for her to go to Llar.'

"Then she took María Luisa by the hand and said, 'Go to Llar, do go.'"

❀   ❀   ❀

"After leaving Montse," Luisa tells, "we cried as we walked the streets. We went into the first church we came across. I could not stop crying and praying. I felt God near me, more intensely than ever.

'You were dying alone,' I wrote in my diary then. 'Everybody dies alone…. But I knew you were peaceful even in the throes of death. You, with your simplicity, had been able to achieve peace. And your peace overflows in joy…. At that moment life had a perfect meaning. You, Lord, were there: it was essential to live for you, much more for you, completely for you. With you life had a precise meaning; without you it had none. Strange: to find the meaning of life through death.'"

❀   ❀   ❀

That night Montse was completely exhausted. She tried to mouth a few words at a quarter to nine. At last her mother managed to understand what she was saying.

"Mom, how hard these little things are!"

"And what do you call these little things?"

"This," Montse said, pointing to her dry mouth.

❀   ❀   ❀

"She could not speak," her mother recalls, "and suffered a horrible thirst but when she tried to drink something, she could not breathe. I remember someone went to fetch her a chocolate ice-cream with which we tried to ease the pain by cooling her lips. But her suffering became more intense. She was like this all night long."

March 26 – Maundy Thursday

Her mother continues: "That night she tried to make herself understood on three occasions. She also made vain attempts to write. We stayed like this until the early hours. I was sitting beside her holding her hand when she asked me, in sign language, to put on the light around our Lady as if saying, 'I want to see her.'

"I was surprised because these lights dazzled her; but she insisted until I did. Then she pointed to the bedside lamp too.

"I was hesitant about switching on all the lights because Montse Amat was at my side, asleep. She had been awake for many nights, but I saw Montse so happy that I left all the lights on for a little while. Then I pointed to Montse Amat who was asleep and, as always, she agreed and I put the lights out."

It was her last renunciation – small but big, at the same time, as all the others had been.

Dawn came. It was a clear early spring day, full of light. She tried to say something at 7 a.m. but neither her parents nor Montse Amat could decipher her efforts. At last they did:

"I am perfectly well."

"What did you say?" her mother asked. "That you are perfectly well?"

"Yes, yes. I dreamt I was trying to say so three times without being able to."

Her mother knelt by her bedside and whispered aspirations into her ear. After a while Montse fell into a peaceful sleep. They brought her an ice-cream to moisten her lips, but she was not able to have it.

The priest from Nuria parish came at 8:30, as he did every morning, to bring her Holy Communion. The previous days he had given her just a sliver as she had mouth ulcers, but she had been able to receive our Lord with the help of a sip of water. Today it was not possible. She could not receive Communion in such a state. Fr. Albert recalls: "I found her profoundly unwell and dizzy. She had her crucifix in her left hand, which she was holding tightly. I stayed for ten minutes and promised to return in a little while."

Lía came soon afterwards. She says: "When I arrived she still recognized me and made signs for me to sit beside her. She asked me to say aspirations as she could not speak.

At 10:00 she woke up and wanted to sit up. She was saying aspirations to our Lady non-stop. I remember her saying: 'My mother, I love you so much! When are you coming to fetch me?'

She kept on kissing her crucifix, which she was unable to take to her mouth unaided. She would throw kisses to our Lady and say over and over again, 'Jesus, Jesus.' She was very agitated. After a while she calmed down. At noon I said the Angelus in her ear. She appeared to hear me and to be praying."

Fernanda Mallorga, Carmen Francés, and Ana María Suriol came and began to pray the rosary quietly.

Her mother recalls: "During the first mystery she had her hands crossed over her breast, with her crucifix as always between them. She appeared to be asleep. At 1:20 p.m., suddenly, just as we were beginning the second mystery, we realized her breathing had changed. Manuel took her pulse. It had disappeared. She grimaced, took three deep breaths... and she left us for heaven."

10

There is no better search

Her body was laid out on the bed wrapped in a white sheet, simple as she was. A garland of white tulips was placed around her body, flowers as cheerful as she was. Rather than losing her life it seemed as if life had come back into her face. She had a peaceful, serene expression, although you could see the marks of suffering. She wore a trace of a smile.

Rosa says: "At that time I thought of how happy Montse had been on earth and how happy she would be in heaven. I remembered how the founder of Opus Dei used to say that the happiness of heaven was for those who knew how to be happy on earth. She was happy, right up to the last moment.

"It seems farfetched, doesn't it? But it is true. She was profoundly happy right up to the last minute, and she made those of us who had the good luck to know her and have dealings with her very happy too, in spite of all her sufferings.... When I meet a customer who is seriously ill in the pharmacy it saddens me, I can't help it. However, she never did make me sad, because the love of God had taken over her soul and she was able to love God above her suffering, her illness, her tragic circumstances... even above death itself."

There was a rose beside the image of Our Lady of Montserrat, beside the palm that Rosa had brought to her on Palm Sunday. There was another red rose on top of her bad leg resting on the sheet. Her Aunt Adela had brought it. It stayed sweet and fresh for two whole days, from the morning of the 26th until the 28th of March, Holy Saturday, the day she was buried.

Her parents, brothers and sisters, and the girls from Llar spent those two nights in vigil beside her. On one of those nights next to his daughter's body, which seemed to be asleep rather than dead, her father said to those present:

"Don't you believe for a minute that this daughter of mine did not know about love. My daughter was in love. She fell in love with God. That was the meaning of her life. That was why she prayed, did apostolate, obeyed, and struggled. I realized she was becoming more and more united with God, struggling constantly, one day after another.... She did all this because she was in love...."

They exchanged her crucifix, the one she handled constantly, for a wooden one, the one that her brother Jorge had made for her. Then they laid her out and put a rose at her feet.

Rosa continues: "When she was taken away I thought of the Christmas carol she loved to sing when Christmas was coming near:

> *There is no better search*
> *Than to look for Christ.*
> *There is no better search*
> *Than to look for Christ...*
> *There just is no better search*"

March 28, 1959

María del Carmen Delclaux recalls: "Montse had made two requests: to put her into the coffin at the last possible moment, and to accompany her to the cemetery. And so we did.

"We buried her in the South-East Cemetery in the oval niche of Via John the Baptist, number 89. It was 9.30 a.m., March 28, Holy Saturday, or Glorious Saturday as we used to call it then, a clear, bright day. It was the 34th anniversary of the priestly ordination of the founder of Opus Dei, which had taken place on March 28, 1925.

Her mother wished to see Montse for the last time. We opened the lid of the coffin and I shall never forget her face there, shining in the sunlight.... The Requiem Mass was celebrated a few days later, on April 4 in the Parish of Our Lady of the Pillar. There was an atmosphere of great serenity, peace, and joy during the ceremony." The parish priest Fr. Vicente Salva on expressing his condolences said, "In a case like this, instead of being sad, we ought to sing Alleluias."

❧   ❧   ❧

The Church began the Process of Inquiry for the Beatification of Montserrat Grases on December 19, 1962, just four years after her death, with the Archbishop of Barcelona, Gregorio Modrego y Casaus, presiding, in the chapel of the Bishop's palace in Barcelona. It was concluded in the church of Our Lady of Montalegre on March 26, 1968, on the 9th anniversary of her death. At 17 most young people are on the threshold of life. However Montse developed so quickly, so much in tune with divine grace, at God's pace, that at this tender age she had arrived, with the simplicity she always displayed, to the fullness of love.

Then the transcript was sent to Rome, to the Congregation for the Causes of Saints. Since then many articles and newsletters have been published about her in different languages: Spanish, French, English, Italian, and Portuguese. An outline of her life, written by Mercedes Eguibar has been reprinted many times.

On February 22, 1974 the Congregation for

the Causes of Saints published a decree on her writings, and on May 15, 1992 the Congregation published the decree proclaiming the validity of the Process.

On October 28, 1993 the auxiliary Bishop of Barcelona, Jaume Traserra, presided at the handing over of the historical documents of the Process to the Congregation of the Causes of Saints for their study.

The prayer card for private devotion to her is as follows:

Prayer

Oh God, you granted your servant Montserrat the grace of serene and cheerful surrender to your Divine Will, lived with admirable simplicity in the midst of the world: Grant that I may know how to lovingly offer you all my daily activities, turning them into a Christian service to others. Deign to glorify your servant and through her intercession grant me the favor I ask of you... (here make your petition). *Amen.*

Our Father. Hail Mary. Glory be to the Father.

❀   ❀   ❀